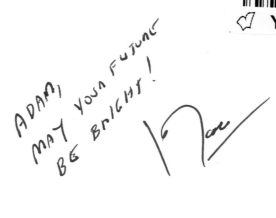

Intended
Consequences

Intended Consequences

Design the Future You Wish to Create

Marc Emmer

Optimize Inc.
24307 Magic Mountain Parkway #368
Valencia, CA 91355

Published by Optimize Inc.

First Edition

Large quantities of this title are available at *www.optimizeinc.net/ic*

ISBN 10 1-4392-4892-3
ISBN 13 9781439248928

Acknowledgements

To our Employees and Advisors:

Paul Butler, Bala Chandrasekhar, Carmela Bertrand, Lori Boyle, Henry DeVries, Alan Gecht, Dan Goetz, Calvin Hedman, Dianne Landau, Lauren Lee, Juliet Mazza, Marilyn Murphy, Mitch Pearlman, Don Riddell, Jim Queen, Lloyd Sreden, Dewayne Sode, Blakey St. John, and Kim Stroh. Your counsel has been invaluable.

Special thanks to our amazing clients including:

Gary Baker, Sam Brown, Dan Byrum, Joe Daquino, Joyce Douglas, Larry Dutra, Ron Georgio, Drew Kaplan, Dan Kravitz, Philip Jones, Mike Kaiser, David Lewis, Steve McDonald, Carmen McRae, David Poole, Steve Saperstein, John Shaffery, Bob Snow, Tim Toomey, and Dale Van Dellen. Your trust in us has meant everything.

To my family, Kerri, Megan and Brooke. You give my life meaning.

Table of Contents

Chapter

1

The Beginning

"Whenever you find yourself on the side of the majority, it is time to pause and reflect."

— MARK TWAIN

This work is intended for entrepreneurs and executives who are entrepreneurial. While I operate a very successful consulting firm, I am at heart an entrepreneur. Entrepreneurs take risks; and we will take some risks in this book. I will endeavor to predict the recipe that will drive competitive advantage over the next decade.

I have committed my company to helping executives see beyond their own assumptions and biases and take control of the future they wish to create. Often that means challenging their limiting beliefs about themselves and their businesses.

Intended Consequences is a compilation of my experiences in the formation of breakthrough strategies, and my observations about how best-in-class companies sustain a competitive advantage. Within the DNA of extraordinary organizations is the ability to manage the tension between creative thought and the structure required to execute strategic initiatives.

The struggle to remain relevant, to engage people to love what they do, and to tie the activities of people to the vision of the organization, is the foundation of our work. While I get paid for assisting companies in building strategic plans and improving profitability, the goals of this book are more transformational. My firm (Optimize Inc.) seeks to ignite thought leadership that will encourage "strategic thinking" as a mantra.

Strategic thinking is a mindset where decisions are made within a framework that supports something larger than the decision itself.

The principles that follow are intended to be provocative in thought, but practical in application. This book presents a model that will assist executives in scripting their ideal future, while engaging others in becoming accountable for the results.

❖   ❖   ❖

The images of US Airways Flight 1549 crash landing into New York's Hudson River will remain permanently etched in our memory. The initial reaction for many was shock. I thought what a fantastic outcome; I wonder what that pilot was thinking?

Pilot Chesley "Sully" Sullenberger, and his crew were flooded with interviews, including an appearance on 60 Minutes. Katie Couric asked the 43-year veteran, "What were some of the things you had to do to make this landing successful?"

Sully: "I needed to touch down with wings exactly level.

I needed to touch down with the nose slightly up.

I needed to touch down with a descent rate that was survivable.

I needed to touch down just above our minimum flying speed, but not below it. And I needed to make all these things happen simultaneously."

Couric: "Was that a hard thing to do?"

Sully: "No, it just took some concentration."

Sullenberger first considered returning to LaGuardia Airport, and then Teterboro in New Jersey. Within a minute of the bird strike that brought down the airliner, Sully had decided that he only had one viable option: to land the plane in the river.

Controller "turn right two-eight-zero, you can land runway one at Teterboro." In the calmest of voices, Sullenberger replied, "We can't do it." Sullenberger had processed Plan A, and Plan B and had moved on to Plan C.

> There is a reason why Sully was so clairvoyant. To process the ramifications so quickly, not only took concentration and focus, but forethought. He had both a checklist and a contingency plan.

Airline pilots are nothing if not vigilant. They are paid to follow a checklist and they work the list every time, without fail, because the cost of failure is just too high. In the case of the "Miracle on the Hudson," Sully clearly had a list he planned on following meticulously, and when it failed to produce the desired result, he quickly moved on to other alternatives.

Foresight seems to be lacking in businesses today, as failed companies such as Lehman Brothers and Bear Stearns were seemingly operating without a contingency plan. We are operating in an economy ripe with disorganization, missed deadlines and failure to meet our commitments. The work environment has become so frantic that there is a free-for-all, often void of real planning. Meanwhile, those rare businesses that employ strategic thinking and commitment to execution (such as Southwest Airlines and Walmart) consistently outpace the competition.

The liquidity crisis of 2008–2009 brought about a spasm in the world-wide economy as a result of converging factors. A by-product of the crisis was that strategic thinking was cast aside in favor of fire fighting.

It was a remarkable irony that some of the sharpest business minds in our economy, such as the leadership at Bear Stearns, Goldman Sachs and General Motors (GM), became so myopic that they did not see the tipping points.

> *Myopia caused the crisis in the first place; and short term thinking beset more short term thinking during the recession that followed.*

My job has been to help businesses build the checklist and come up with the contingency plan. It takes a special talent to maintain strategic focus and discipline. It is the few, not the many, who meet their potential in this way.

Success is a dangerous tonic; it leads people to assume that the activities and strategies that lead to their success will be the same ones that will enable them to get where they want to go. The growth of most businesses follows the familiar S Curve, similar to a product life cycle. Through the life of a company, there are stages of growth followed by periods of stagnation as the company retools with new infrastructure, systems and human capital. As a company evolves, there must be re-alignment and accountability to a different set of directives.

Thus even highly successful, highly profitable companies can lose their way quickly. With achievement along the S Curve comes complacency. People are easily conditioned to accept the status quo and can feel threatened when prompted to consider new ideas.

In February of 2004, Coca-Cola announced that CEO Douglas Daft would be retiring in December of that year. The announcement came as a surprise to the markets which expected Daft to serve well into retirement age. The greater shock came several weeks later when the Coke Board announced that the company's President and COO, Steve Heyer, would not succeed Daft as Chief Executive.

The Board elaborated that Heyer did not have the "leadership abilities" to run the company (he evidently had the leadership skills to be the #2 executive, but not the #1). Furthermore, the Board announced that they were reviewing "external candidates" because none of Coca-Cola's 100,000+ employees had the necessary skill sets to lead the company.

Heyer abruptly resigned that September. In the course of three months, Coca-Cola, had lost its top two executives. Something at Coke was terribly wrong and the markets reacted harshly.

Just three months after Coke's announcement, McDonald's CEO Jim Cantalupo had a massive heart attack and died suddenly at the company's franchise convention in Orlando, Florida. McDonald's stature as one of the world's most respected companies had plummeted in recent years. Armed with a new menu and commitment to standards, Cantalupo had revived the company.

McDonald's Board, understanding the gravity of the situation, held an emergency meeting. Within hours of Cantalupo's death, Charlie Bell, the company's President and Chief Operating Officer, was elevated to President and CEO. An announcement was made before the opening bell the following Monday.

Bell mused to friends that "we have such clarity in our mission and strategy, it really doesn't matter who is CEO." Later that year, Mr. Bell was diagnosed with cancer and resigned in November to concentrate on fighting his illness. He died two months later.

In the 18 months following Coke's announcement, the food sector performed well, but Coke's share price remained principally unchanged. In the same 18 month span, McDonald's share price soared 26% even after losing its top two executives.[1]

While there are a multitude of factors that contribute to the ebbs and flows of any stock price, it is pretty clear Wall Street felt more confident about McDonald's prospects than it did about Coca-Cola's, and the upheaval of Coke's senior management had to be a mitigating factor.

Coke's Board, managing the world's largest beverage operation, did not have enough forethought to plan thoughtfully for succession and their business valuation suffered. It appears that Coke's Board and senior management lacked clarity of purpose and organizational alignment. In McDonald's case, the Board's actions and the consequences of those actions demonstrated clear intent.

While shocking, the disconnect at Coke was only mildly surprising. To lead in times of volatility and hyper-competitiveness, leaders need real time, unfiltered information about the performance of the organization and the people who serve within it.

There is a litmus test that I like to use to decipher if alignment exists within an organization: ask your top five managers to access or write down your top five strategic priorities and see how many can name all five.

> *It is as if great companies have some type of secret sauce, some corporate DNA, that promotes superior and sustainable business results, year after year.*

> *Therein lies the opportunity to unleash value: to create companies that are so well positioned and so resilient that they remain relevant regardless of economic and industry conditions.*

Success does not happen by accident, best-in-class companies are intentional in the disruptions they create. They are intentional about the type of people they hire and in the expectations they set for them. They convert their strategy into clearly articulated objectives that are interwoven into their way of doing business.

Exceptional companies are the exception. What is it in the corporate Kool-Aid that allows McDonald's to be so consistent in their food product and management? Why does Intel out-innovate their competition? Why does Nordstrom provide better service, time after time? Most importantly, how will your corporate DNA provide the impetus for sustainable competitive advantage?

What is your secret sauce? The substance of this book is about creating a unique selling proposition and then leveraging that strategic advantage to create an extraordinary company. Building an extraordinary company affords the entrepreneur the opportunity to be in complete control of his or her life.

One important caveat: this book blends distinctly different ways of viewing the world. Strategy is highly intangible. It is as much art as it is science. Execution of strategy is far more structured and requires discipline. This book endeavors to blend the vision of what we can't see with the reality of what we must see.

The methodology presented follows a logical progression:

1. An organization needs to have a clear vision that defines what its ideal future looks like (strategy). Further, in the dynamic marketplace, the strategy must be flexible enough to adapt to market conditions. It must also be relevant and provocative in a world where differentiation and unique customer experiences are difficult to deliver and sustain.

2. Results-oriented companies define what they hold people accountable to.

3. In order to create exceptional experiences, companies must have the most talented people (who will be increasingly harder to come by in the next decade).

4. Scorecards can be leveraged to enable better efficiency, quality, service and fulfillment of strategic initiatives.

5. When tied back to scorecards (and the strategy), performance management systems (including incentives) create alignment between successful companies and their employees.

6. The loop must be repeated every year, as the strategy is molded, crafted and reengineered based on changing market conditions.

You will observe that many of the examples used are for well known global brands, many of them business to consumer (B2C). It is important to accept that these examples are equally relevant to the small company as to the large. Customer's expectations of vendors are the same, whether or not the smaller company has the resources to offer similar services. To ignore these principles out of a belief that they are only germane to large organizations would minimize your return on investment in this book.

> *Small companies can learn a lot by examining the best practices of larger companies, or at least can think deeply about how to counteract them. In the sport of Judo, one participant uses the energy of their opponent against them, and often the smaller opponent wins.*

While I do not claim to have some crystal ball that can see the future, this book will demonstrate that one can predict elements of the future with some accuracy. In order to offer a framework for competitive advantage in the next decade, the following chapters will offer some projections, based on facts already in evidence today.

I had another important motivation to bring about this work. I believe that the US liquidity crisis and deep recession that followed was in part a result of faulty assumptions about risk. By 2008, the world's top financial institutions such as Morgan Stanley and Merrill Lynch reported asset to capital ratios of roughly 25:1. Bank of America's bank leverage ratio was 73:1. Complex hedging investments made by such institutions masked their exposure. All that was necessary was a moderate drop in asset values for these companies to cascade out of control.[2]

The acceptance of overleverage by the banking system, coupled with inflated real estate values shaped our concept of normalcy. We have come to accept a level of growth in our economy based on a flawed set of assumptions.

We have been forced to accept new realities, not based on temporary cycles but permanent changes to the marketplace. Business leaders must challenge the assumptions made by the experts, the economists and the business press. We will pay an onerous price for the massive US stimulus package, including a massive Federal debt which could exceed 100% of the GNP within a decade. I challenge the assumption by many that things will just go back to the way they were. Wealth will be harder to create in the next decade than it was in the last. Companies will have to be better equipped to compete in the days ahead.

Both strategy and execution are more important than they have ever been.

❖   ❖   ❖

A note to our readers:

Statistically speaking, most people do not read books cover to cover. We hope you will make an exception. If you choose to scan the book we have provided key concepts in "call outs" throughout as well as chapter reviews at the end of each chapter.

The first half of this book is conceptual, providing insight on how to create a killer value proposition. Chapter 10 provides a "how to guide" for strategic planning. The remainder of the book focuses on execution, featuring a unique take on scorecarding and metrics (Chapter 11 is a must read). Let the fun begin!

Chapter

2

Strategic Thinking as a Mantra

"The future ain't what it used to be."

— Yogi Berra

B EING AN OWNER OR CEO is the ultimate responsibility in a business, and there are a host of emotions that come along with it. I have had business owners share the sheer joy of achieving success, riches and independence, and have seen others simply break down, petrified that they will lose it all.

> Great management teams have candid conversations based on the brutal, unbridled truth. As a result, they are able to be more nimble. They can move toward new products, markets, methodologies and systems because they are not afraid of upsetting the apple cart.

One of the most important lessons I have learned as a trusted advisor to senior executives is that they appreciate candor. As a strategy practitioner, that means challenging the underlying assumptions about the business. I cannot afford to be politically correct; that is someone else's job.

It is often lonely at the top. Most senior executives have very few people to talk to. They are often unwilling to have crucial conversations with Board members and employees are unwilling to have crucial conversations with them. So, they talk to people like me.

It takes a great deal of emotional intelligence and trust to engage in open debate. The best leaders are also willing to fail. Former Proctor & Gamble CEO A. G. Lafley said, "You learn more from failure...but the key is to fail early, fail cheaply, and don't make the same mistake twice."

The most dynamic CEOs surround themselves with direct reports and advisors who are willing to challenge their thinking and take risks. The old school executives who are caught up in ego are not long for a world where irrelevance is easy to come by. To compete in today's environment requires a mindset where no product, service, department, employee or methodology is off limits.

> *Companies must confront the change that confronts them. The question that every senior manager should ask is, "Will our business be relevant a year from now?" The great Peter Drucker once asked GE CEO Jack Welch, "If you weren't already in this business, would you enter it today?"*

Many senior executives live in fear because they do not believe they are in control of forces that could dictate their success or failure. And in fact, often they are not. Others live in denial that their sheer will is enough for their company to prosper, regardless of outside forces that could have a material effect on their profitability.

Best-in-class companies are externally focused and they are thinking about the future all the time. Amazon is an example of a company adept at finding white spaces (competing against noncompetition) while also expanding the markets they already serve. Amazon has an extraordinary record of making long term wagers that have paid off.

Amazon's founder Jeff Bezos has woven strategic thinking into the fabric of the company. "We are willing to plant seeds and wait a long time for them to turn into trees. The important question to ask is, is it big enough to be meaningful to the company as a whole if we're very successful?[3] It helps to base your strategy on things that won't change."

When asked by *Harvard Business Review* about Amazon's service model, Bezos said, "It's that our customers who are buyers are very convenience motivated. We make it really, really easy to buy things. You can see that if you look at a metric like our revenue per click or revenue per page turn. It's very high because we're efficient for people."[4] Amazon uses operational measurements to track execution against its core business strategy, which has been derived from customer insights.

"Do we have the will and the vision to be in the business that is replacing us?"

To maintain focus on long term initiatives, senior Amazon executives attend a strategic off-site annually and dedicate four hours every Tuesday to monitoring progress versus long term initiatives. As a result, Amazon did not just innovate in creating the Web distribution for everything from books and CDs to appliances, the company has engaged in a continuous wave of innovation, slashing prices, expanding selection and making shopping online easier. Kindle is revolutionizing the book business; much in the way that iPod did the music industry.

Disruptive innovation is rare because we form opinions based on our own biases. We defend our biases ruthlessly from any contradictory view. In politics, our views have become so polarized that many liberals will not even consider conservative points of view, and vice versa.

Yet the greatest thinkers in history, such as Einstein, Newton and Galileo, spent most of their lives consumed with finding evidence that would disprove their own theories. This seems counter to our thinking because of what philosophers refer to as "confirmation bias" or our tendency to seek out information that validates our opinions versus those that provide a counterargument.[5]

It may not shock you that as a strategist, my favorite board game is chess. One of the attributes that separates great chess players from poor players is that the master will consider bizarre combinations of moves which will include the sacrificing of pieces to achieve checkmate. The novice will summarily eliminate these combinations from consideration because they cannot project far enough ahead to see the strategic advantage gained by creating any short term disadvantage.

The first five or six moves of the game played by white (the player that moves first) are somewhat scripted (known as a gambit). The master knows every possible combination of moves that the opponent will make to counteract the gambit. In other words, the scenarios are clear to him, and he knows exactly how to play them to secure the ideal positioning. By the middle of the game, he uses his vision and creativity to expose his opponent's weaknesses.

Creativity in business is hampered by both hard and soft barriers to change. We are trained in business school to mitigate risks. Thus, businesses systematically create functional departments such as accounting, sales and operations and give them the authority to protect their territory as a defense mechanism.

So how is it that the most brilliant business minds of our time, such as the leadership at Bear Stearns and Goldman Sachs, were completely ill prepared for the liquidity crisis? The answer can be found in a metaphor provided by Nassim Nicholas Taleb in *The Black Swan,* his witty deluge into "The Impact of the Highly Improbable"[6]:

> *"Consider a turkey that is fed every day. Every single feeding will firm up the bird's belief that it is the general rule of life to be fed every day by friendly members of the human race, looking out for its best interests. On the afternoon of the Wednesday before Thanksgiving, something unexpected will happen to the turkey. It will incur a revision of belief."*

Our body produces Dopamine, which as Taleb eludes to, is proven to regulate the chemistry of the brain in such a way as to create patterns in our thinking which minimize randomness. In other words, we are predisposed to think of things in terms of recurring events, and it is alien for us to think of things that do not fit into a logical pattern. This is why we panic during disasters, not only because of the fear of the unknown, but because our mind cannot reconcile events we have not experienced before such as an earthquake or car accident.

The only plausible explanation for the liquidity crisis and the giant sucking sound that followed is that contrary viewpoints about the stability of our systems and our markets were not properly considered, and that oversight cost our economy trillions of dollars and millions of jobs.

> *Humans are wired to attach ourselves to patterns that we expect to continue and we avoid open, frank discussions about what will change. It is not that we are merely resistant to change; it is that considering information that does not fit a pattern requires more energy for us to process. It is actually more strenuous to our body chemistry to consider alternatives.*

Being on the cusp of the baby boom generation, about the worst things my peers and I experienced growing up were early memories of Martin Luther King's assassination, the Challenger accident and perhaps the Boston Celtics beating the Los Angeles Lakers in the 1984 championship series (for the record, the Lakers got them back in '85 and '87).

People of my generation grew up with a relative level of stability. We are not accustomed to much variability, a concept that was rocked on September 11, 2001. It was not only the loss of life and the realization that sects of people hated Americans to such a degree that shocked so many of us: it was that we felt the safety of our borders was threatened, a notion completely incongruent with the pattern we had known since we were young.

Upon reflection, 9/11 taught us a painful yet meaningful life lesson: we often don't understand the gravity of a situation while we are watching it unfold. When my wife first called me at my office that September morning and told me a plane had hit the World Trade Center, my initial reaction was disbelief. I remember uttering the words, "You mean like a small plane; like a turboprop, right?"

The consequences of the liquidity crisis were eerily similar. Most of us did not understand the magnitude of the problem until it was too late. There are enormous business ramifications within the concept of variability. We can be lulled to sleep by our access to capital, the stability of our markets and the satisfaction of our customers.

In the pages to follow we will present ideas on how to reduce variability and the business risk associated with it.

Chapter 2 Review

- Human beings are wired to seek out patterns. It is human nature to be myopic and have biases that cloud our vision. Great leaders surround themselves with people who challenge their thinking.

- Few companies innovate because they are not capable of challenging their own assumptions. Seek out people who are willing to make counterintuitive bets.

- Well run companies employ strategic thinking all the time and dedicate time to long-term planning and execution.

Chapter

3

The Forces Around Us

*"The only constant is change, continued
change, inevitable change."*

— Isaac Asimov

Having facilitated dozens of strategic planning sessions, my experience has been that most companies are internally focused. That is, they spend an extraordinary amount of time thinking about their existing initiatives, and how they can extend their current offering to gain incremental revenue or profit.

Imagine you were a record executive in 2002. Evidently, the brass at Time Warner Music and Sony were thinking about how they could produce and distribute more CDs at big box retailers like Walmart and Best Buy, and music retailers such as Sam Goody and Tower Records. Their focus was to fend off competition within their narrowly defined market space.

It was as if the industry had some type of collective myopia (short sightedness) that clouded their ability to consider external factors that would affect their long term horizon. They simply didn't see the tipping point:

- Moore's Law (Intel's Geoffrey Moore's assertion that computer processing speed would double every 18 months while prices would remain constant or fall) had proven to be true. Our economy transitioned from dial up to broadband as the primary delivery system for the Internet and the ability to compress large files was born.
- As chip manufacturers produced smaller, lighter and cheaper chips, the cost of electronic devices fell sharply creating a marketplace for PDAs and MP3 players.

- Social trends brought about our burgeoning individualism, the precursor to social networking sites such as My Space, Facebook, Twitter, and LinkedIn.
- The United States and other governments offered little regulation for e-Commerce on the Internet.
- Within the music industry, record executives feared the loss of intellectual capital through file sharing on sites such as Napster.

The series of events can be illustrated in a Futures Map:

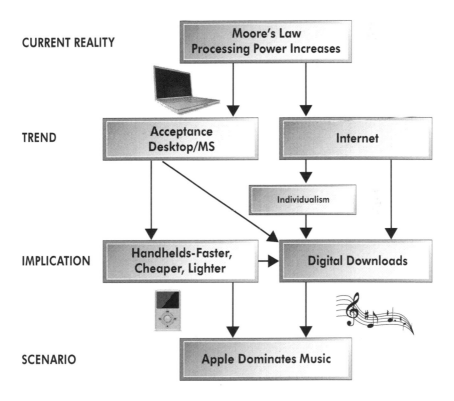

This recipe created an environment where an outsider, a computer maker, dismantled an industry (in about three years) that took 70 years to erect.

There are times when powerful outside forces move an industry with little pretense or warning. The wine industry has experienced two watershed events in the last 20 years. In 1991, the 60 Minutes "French Paradox" episode (which alluded to a potential correlation to the consumption of red wine and the lower incidence of heart disease in some European countries) was the impetus to a massive spike in wine sales. A decade passed before the next industry game changer. In the quirky independent film "Sideways" the lead character (Miles) made clear his disdain for Merlot (the most consumed red wine grape in the US at the time) when he quipped, "If anyone orders Merlot, I'm leaving. I am not drinking any [expletive] Merlot." The film took on a cult following and received much critical acclaim. Within three months, A. C. Nielsen reported a 15% spike in Pinot Noir sales (after a 3 year decline), as demand for Merlot plummeted.[7]

Regions that grew Pinot Noir grapes (such as Santa Barbara's Santa Ynez region where "Sideways" was filmed, and Oregon's Coastal Region) were flooded with tourists through a phenomena known as "The Sideways Effect."

> *From the evolution of the iPod, to the acceptance of Pinot Noir, and the ratings spike of televised sports as a result of HDTV, examples abound of markets that are materially altered as a result of factors external to the industry.*

Myopia can spread in the form of conventional wisdom, which could be viewed as "collective myopia." What makes collective myopia so remarkable is that it seems to inflict entire industries as in the case of the financial services industry whose strategists all took on similar assumptions about risk and access to liquidity.

On February 20, 2003, the rock band Great White was performing at The Station, a Rhode Island night club. The band opened with a pyrotechnic display. Within moments, the club was engulfed in fire, spreading toxic fumes.

As 450 occupants attempted to flee the club, most attempted to leave through the door they came in, following the crowd (herding) and not seeking out any of the other four exits. One hundred people died that night, 40 of them just outside the exit where they were wedged in the doorway.

Herding in the financial markets can be devastating. The advent of the Internet and real time information has enabled the phenomena, allowing communities to swell in a matter of hours, and move in a given direction.

> *Collective myopia's evil cousin is "herding": the need for people and markets to be influenced by the few, and blindly follow in their footsteps.*

Herding had a causal effect in the financial sector in the form of credit default swaps and other exotic financial instruments that led to a meltdown in 2008. As of 2006, the value of derivatives around the world was $473 trillion, while the combined value of the stocks and bonds on which those derivatives were based were worth only a combined $119 trillion.[8] Meaning that worldwide capital markets were not much more than a Bernard Madoff Ponzi scheme, and the deck of cards had to crumble eventually.

As we will illustrate in Chapter 4, the strategist must consider cycles in the context of converging factors (such as regulation and liquidity) which may occur in various combinations and materially affect a business or industry. The future of any business is a complex chain of variables that cannot be ignored.

❖ ❖ ❖

What future do you want to create?

Chapter 3 Review

- Most companies are internally focused and do not consider factors external to their industry.

- Tipping points occur when a convergence of factors are the impetus to change.

- Entire industries can be affected by "collective myopia" and "herding" in a particular direction as evidenced by the collapse of the global financial markets. Be conscious of these tendencies and consider the possibility of seemingly random events.

Chapter

4

The Strategist's Ace in the Hole: Scenario Planning

"The reason why most people face the future with apprehension instead of anticipation is because they don't have it well designed."

— JIM ROHN

It is ironic that our business success in large part is based on our ability to forecast a future which is impossible to predict accurately. That is exactly the reason companies should invest more time in an effort to plan for such eventualities. Like a forecast or budget, a scenario does not need to come true to be worth conceiving.

In his book, *Inevitable Surprises,* Peter Schwartz points out that the Hart-Rudman Commission scenario plan "anticipated terrorists would destroy the World Trade Center by crashing airliners into it. These forces are what scenario planners call predetermined elements, forces that we can anticipate with certainty because we already see their early stages in the world today. They are also going to surprise us because, while the basic events are virtually predetermined, the timing, results and consequences are not."

Scenario Planning is a methodology where possible scenarios and potential tipping points are schemed and prodded. Scenario Planning is usually precluded by a STEEP Analysis. In conducting this exercise, a catalog of conceivable **S**ocial, **T**echnological, **E**conomic, **E**cological and **P**olitical trends are assembled. Then the participants rank the probability of each predication and create the most pessimistic, and optimistic set of scenarios. The greatest probability is that the reality will fall somewhere in-between.

One could wonder, will we ever return to normalcy, or
is normalcy a concept from a past era? Has volatility
become the norm?

The once predictable business cycle has become highly disrupted. In just one decade, the US economy has been mired with Y2K, 9/11, the wars in Iraq and Afghanistan, the Asian Financial Crisis (and Bird Flu), Katrina, Tsunamis, Mad Cow, Enron and WorldCom (and the madness of the Sarbanes-Oxley Act of 2002 that followed), the US liquidity crisis, and triple-digit fluctuations in energy and raw materials prices. Volatility has become the norm.

That is why scenarios must be considered, debriefed and planned. It is beyond comprehension that Countrywide, IndyMac and other subprime lenders did not have a contingency plan for the possibility of a collapse of the US housing market (which finally happened in 2007–2008), that US airlines did not prepare for volatile oil prices (beginning in 2007), or that US automobile manufacturers were not prepared for a spike in demand of fuel efficient cars.

The master strategist does not presume to know the future. Yet time after time, those companies who have thought through future events are more prepared for the inevitable. Strategic thinking cannot be done in a vacuum. To promote a strategic viewpoint, organizational structures, capital structures, company culture, etc. must be built from the ground up to support the execution of strategy and potential market volatility. The quest to understand the possibilities uncovers important learning about vendors, competitors, customers and markets.

Companies often make failed assumptions about what the market will bare based on our bias and emotions. For years, computer manufacturers have been trying to pack more features and speed into laptop computers, while trying to price them in a range slightly higher than desktops. Those assumptions where challenged in the One Laptop per Child initiative (the goal to develop the $100 laptop for children of developing countries).

Asustek, a Taiwanese computer maker, developed a stripped down Internet ready version of an ultra light computer, using Linux and a tiny 7 inch screen.[9] In relative terms, the computer was slow, and had few applications.

The product was the antithesis of everything perceived as a need in the marketplace, and thus marketers were shocked that the early adopters of the product were middle class consumers. And thus the "Netbook" was born. It turns out that there are a lot of people who only require a single icon on their computer; the one with their Internet browser. Instead of hardware innovation trickling down from high end to low, a new generation of computers were established on the low end and then sold upstream to consumers who were thought to want more features.

Emotions govern our thinking on many levels. The electronic age has brought new volatility to markets, and has created a fertile environment for both arbitrage by institutional types, and droves of individual investors moving in unison to support some conventional wisdom about energy prices, gold, or the stock price of Intel or Apple. It is as if our economy is a large rubber band susceptible to large swings based in part on consumer confidence. Our tendency to overreact to stimuli is a form of collective euphoria or despair.

Our thinking often crystallizes around "the economic cycle" which cannot be evaluated independently. The economy is merely a component of a spider web of stressors that can be deeply affected by social, economic, cultural, political and military events.

US history is riddled with periods of growth and decline steered by the mood of the nation. After the panic and fear of the Great Depression, and World War II, the United States settled into a period of profound optimism and growth. They were happy days in America, as the Wonder Bread/Leave it to Beaver era reigned in conformity and stability.

With scant warning, the JFK assassination inflicted a deep wound, a precursor to two decades of volatility and violence, as our nation slid into a deep funk. It took twenty years for the pendulum to swing back again. On the heels of the US hockey team Gold Medal in the 1980 Olympics, Ronald Reagan proclaimed it was "morning in America" during his State of the Union in 1984 alluding to the nation's restored optimism.[10]

The Dow Jones Industrial Average shot up by a factor of eight times from 1982 to 2000 only to lose half its value between 2000 and 2008 as the market crashed again.[11] A similar bubble occurred in oil futures, with oil reaching $145 per barrel in July in 2008, only to fall within a year to trade in the $50 range. Clearly, bubbles represent investors overreacting to markets and accepting a new perception of normalcy and a different tolerance for risk.

In *Animal Spirits,* George Akerlof, and Robert Shiller point out that the 2008–2009 recession mirrored the two that preceded it (1991 and 2001) both in terms of the converging factors that initiated them, and the emotional response that followed.

In both cases, scandals mired the financial markets adding to the severity of the contraction. In the early '90s the S&L debacle followed deregulation. In the form of the Resolution Trust Corp., the US government took on the burden of bad Savings and Loan debt. During the recession of 2001, Arthur Anderson folded after failing to provide oversight in its audit of the defunct Enron, creating the impetus for The Sarbanes-Oxley Act of 2002. In 2008, history repeated itself.

Alan Greenspan's reference to "irrational exuberance" was code for saying, you're all crazy to be paying these prices for real estate and stocks, and the market is going to spasm. Greenspan himself got caught up in the fervor, allowing the credit market to overextend itself based on the false premise that poor controls on derivatives were acceptable as long as the underlying assets (housing prices) continued to increase.

In poker, once a player has made several bets to a hand, he will often seek to protect his emotional and monetary investment by continuing to bet, even though the odds are no longer in his favor. This is a tendency known as being "pot committed." Whether it be investing in chips, oil or a new product line, our emotions can get the best of us.

Decision making should always be based on current and future realities and not based on past investments. The strategist must consider a complex weave of mitigating factors (internal and external) from an objective (non-emotional) standpoint and shape informed assumptions based on a balanced assessment of vulnerability and risk.

❖   ❖   ❖

During my travels on the national speaking circuit, I have had the opportunity to pose questions to more than 1,000 senior executives about their fundamental business issues. My modus operandi includes asking them what their most pressing business problems are. Typically the same issues come up again and again:

- Margins are eroding
- My customers expect the best quality, the lowest price, quick turnaround time and outstanding service
- I can't build infrastructure fast enough
- I can't hire and retain the best people
- It is hard to hold people accountable to specific outcomes
- There is a disconnect between the people who build the strategy and those responsible for executing it

Global hyper-competition has brought about massive cost cutting (off shoring and outsourcing) and an emphasis on efficiency (lean manufacturing, Six Sigma). Cheap communication has shrunk the globe. The business environment is very challenging and at an apex, where it will become more difficult to create differentiation and fend off commoditization.

The concept of singular "business cycle" is a fallacy, as businesses are working within four distinct cycles:

Business Cycle — The ebb and flow of various economic factors including the stock market.

Monetary Cycle — The manipulation of money supply, currency fluctuations (and the effect on imports/exports), and interest rates by central banks (generally in an effort to balance inflation and unemployment).

Industry Cycle — Dynamic changes in supply and demand within an industry, often driven by disruptive innovations and technologies that change the competitive landscape. External factors can drive substantial change such as the effect that Sarbanes-Oxley had on finance and accounting (regulation is often cyclical). In technology, waves of innovation are typical, as the case of massive investments that take place around the release of a new Microsoft operating system, or a new generation of wireless technologies (the next big technology wave will be a combination of these two innovations as new cell phone operating systems allow enhanced functionality).

Company S Curve — The familiar phases of growth and stagnation for companies as they outgrow their infrastructure, processes and talent.

Here is an example of how a hypothetical company might develop visual depiction of the future (it would be bad form to print an actual client's Futures Map, even with their permission):

Assume we have done significant research on behalf of the fictional Z Vitamin Company. A STEEP Analysis yields us the following variables and trends to consider:

- The company believes it can grow quickly while targeting the Baby Boomers who prefer natural products to prescriptions drugs for treating ailments such as high cholesterol, aching joints and arthritis.
- After three years of losses, the company lost its credit line. The company is not yet bankable in any material way and will need access to capital to grow. Short term cash flow must be optimized.
- The company needs to create a call center, but with a lack of funding to hire full time people and a costly facility, the company has opted in the short term to create a virtual call center (a growth area in call centers for companies such as Jet Blue).
- Consumer research reveals that more than a third of the company's clients will respond to marketing that demonstrates that the company uses recycled materials.
- The company will employ a two-pronged strategy to acquire customers: Z Vitamin will launch an aggressive campaign to position as subject matter experts in consumer magazines and on television; the company will hire a medical doctor as their spokesman.

- A recent search engine optimization project (SEO) yielded unexpected results. The company believes augmenting its Internet offering with the call center will generate significant consumer direct volume.
- The company will lean out its operations and outsource large shipments to a supplier who can offer drop shipments of a single item at low-cost. The company will still ship the more complex orders and custom formulations but will need to do so more efficiently with a shorter cycle time.

The process for conducting a STEEP Exercise is described in Chapter 10. After conducting a STEEP Analysis and other research, Z Vitamin could develop a Futures Map.

A Futures Map is a powerful instrument for communicating strategic vision to visual thinkers (about half of the population). Within one document, the strategist can communicate the goals of the organization and roadmap for achieving competitive advantage.

Following is an oversimplified example:

To interpret unrelated combinations of events, economic and otherwise, marks the DNA of a visionary. In October 2007, DuPont CEO Chad Holliday was visiting a customer in Japan, who complained of poor conditions there, and the effect declining demand was having on his cash flow. Upon his return to the US Holliday heard that automakers, (who order paint from DuPont only 48 hours before applying it to new vehicles) were dramatically curbing production.[12]

Holliday put two and two together and did not waste any time. The following morning, Holliday deployed the company's "Crisis Management" plan, employing 17 teams to attack the problem, which in Holliday's eyes was the likelihood that the company's business was about to erode quickly. Within 10 days, every DuPont employee met with a manager to re-clarify expectations and re-direct the company's resources. Chad Holliday, much like Sully Sullenberger, had a checklist and a contingency plan.

A scenario plan, as illustrated in the Z Vitamin Futures Map, that blends potential external factors (beyond our control) with internal initiatives to create a roadmap for the future the client *intends* to create. We do not know, with complete certainty that events will unfold as we planned, but by having specific and relevant predictive indicators, we can measure the accuracy of our scenario plan and make adjustments as needed. We can also build multiple budgets based upon multiple scenarios.

Scenario plans provide unique insights about the future, so that an organization can attempt to predict future events and preempt new markets. Consider some scenarios that are likely to occur in the next 10–20 years:[13]

- A global fresh water shortage and drought conditions emerge in both developed and undeveloped countries.
- Nanotechnologies (materials and machines one billionth of a meter) provide extraordinary breakthroughs such as artificial intelligence so sophisticated, you cannot differentiate between talking to a human or a machine.

- Dramatic changes in medicine eliminate the need for most invasive surgeries. Stem cell research allows for natural replacement of teeth and organic material.
- Insurance companies gain the ability to conduct predictive modeling of consumers and predict future ailments based on lifestyle choices, captured in real time. Health care becomes the pervasive issue driving American socio-economics.
- The expansion of counterfeiting is rampant, creating a cashless society.
- Explosive inflation of prices for natural resources such as nickel, copper, zinc and coal lead to development of the Antarctic and other untapped resources.
- A significant food borne illness kills thousands of people and threatens the food supply.
- Leading oil producing countries such as Saudi Arabia shift resources to solar power, thereby leveraging the extreme climate to produce clean and sustainable energy at low-cost (it has been asserted that like Moore's Law, every time the volume of solar output doubles, the cost is reduced 20%).[14]
- The US builds "smart infrastructure" including smart roads and smart grids that control the flow of traffic, identify bridge failures, etc.
- New economic realities:
  - Shareholder contempt leads to significant changes in corporate tax law and governance. Government agencies are reorganized to provide much stricter oversight.
  - Much higher tax rates for individuals earning more than $250,000 per year, with the highest marginal rates as high as 40%.
  - Leverage ratios of less than 20 to 1.
  - GNP growth of 1–3% per annum.
  - Unemployment hovers around 10%.
- The drastic and real possibility is that the US government could take on even more extraordinary national debt (as high has 100% of the GNP by 2019), or even default. At the very least, there are prospects for long term devaluing of

the US dollar which is likely to lead to the return of sharply higher energy prices (we are a decade or more away from converting to renewable energy). The failing of the Social Security and Medicare systems will put more pressure on the Baby Boom generation to redirect their investments, potentially straining global markets and liquidity.

❖   ❖   ❖

Does your company have a contingency plan?

Chapter 4 Review

⟡ Scenario Planning is a methodology whereby the strategist tries to predict future events.

⟡ A STEEP Exercise is a tool for considering how Social, Technological, Economic, Ecological and Political factors may affect a business in the future.

⟡ The "business cycle" is a misnomer, as every business is operating within monetary, economic, industry and its own growth (S Curve).

⟡ A Futures Map is an illustration of a scenario and can be used with employees, vendors or customers to explain the company's vision for the future.

Chapter
5
Strategy as an Evolution

*"The trouble in America is not that
we are making too many mistakes,
but that we are making too few."*

— PHILIP KNIGHT

Our client, Gothic Landscape, ranks in the top 100 commercial landscapers in the United States. Gothic's business was built around new housing development and is highly cyclical. In anticipation of future downturns, the company established Gothic Grounds Management in 2002 to provide ongoing maintenance to HOA's and the like. In doing so, Gothic created a hedge and passive income stream that reduced the risk of market volatility.

At about the same time, another client, Adams Wine Group, purchased the Adler Fels Winery in Sonoma, California. Adler Fels is a leader in the production of private and control label wines.

During the construction collapse in 2008, Gothic Grounds Management was a stabilizing force and primary generator of cash as the company weathered the storm, unlike many of their competitors who suffered extraordinary financial losses. During the downturn in the broader economy that followed, Adler Fels capitalized on more consumers drinking lower priced wines at home at a time when Adams Wine Group's core business softened.

It was through forethought and planning that these companies strengthened their financial position and were prepared for the eventual marketplace volatility that was so disruptive to many of their competitors. Only after looking outward and understanding the market forces that govern the marketplace can companies focus on internal factors.

The greatest hurdle for most organizations (in terms of our work) is simply committing adequate time and resources to the discipline of planning. Richard Rumelt, Professor at Anderson School of Management at the University of California Los Angeles, said, "Most corporate strategic plans have little to do with strategy. They are simply three year rolling resource budgets and some sort of market share projection. Calling this strategic planning creates false expectations that the exercise will somehow produce a coherent strategy."[15]

Why are companies so consumed with short term, tactical thinking? Stephen Covey's four quadrants come to mind. Companies spend an extraordinary amount of time reacting, based upon what is urgent and not important instead of working on what is important and not urgent.

Imagine that the time expended to complete the work within an organization (your collective bandwidth) was illustrated in a pie. A portion of that time is spent planning, the remainder is spent reacting. The greater the time spent planning, the smaller the pie.

Say you were a small company with five senior managers and 100 employees. Assuming a 40 hour work week and 50 weeks per year, the collective labor investment is 200,000 work hours. At the very least, isn't it logical that one would want to spend a couple of days a year planning (5 executives x 16 hours = 80 hours) and prioritizing how you will expend the other 199,920 hours? The same math applies whether you have 50 employees or 5,000.

Strategic planning is the impetus for a multitude of activities that deliver shareholder value. The strategy should be the basis for everything from departmental goal setting, to KPIs and performance management.

A framework for strategic planning and execution could be illustrated as:

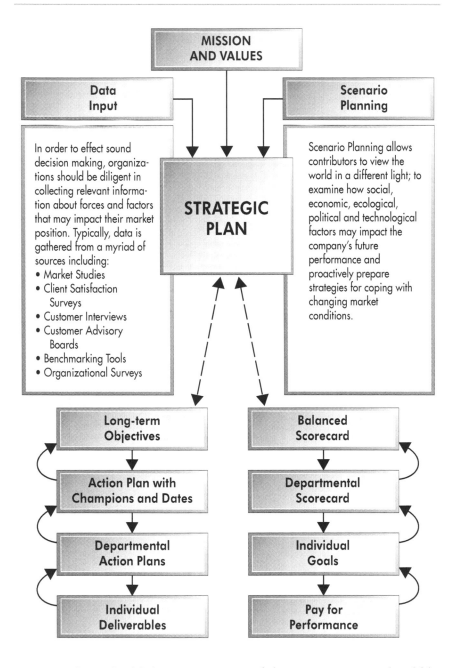

In order to build the most meaningful output, strategy should be based on meaningful input. Data collected in the development of a strategy must be vetted so that valid assumptions are made.

In preparation for Strategic Planning, external data (economic data, industry trends, etc.) should be gathered and reassessed, even if it was analyzed in the recent past.

Internal	External
Employee Surveys	Market Intelligence
Customer Surveys	Supplier Feedback
Financial Statements	Government Statistics
Marketing ROI Analysis	Industry/Trade Statistics
Market Segmentation	Blogs/Trade Press
KPIs	Trade Associations
Web Traffic	Competitive Web Sites
Customer Advisory Boards	Competitive Web Traffic
Surveys of Non Customers	Benchmarking

Perhaps the central question that must always be addressed in strategic planning is what businesses should our company participate in? Criteria to consider include:

- Is there adequate business volume (supply and demand) to sustain business growth? (Webvan seemed like such a good idea at the time.)
- Are the products or services offered commoditized, or could they be viable with slight modifications in the delivery/service model?
- Are there high barriers to entry or is scale obtainable so that others cannot produce similar products at a similar price? (This situation is generally reserved for the largest or most technically capable suppliers.)
- Does the business have access to operating capital, through the sale of stock or external sources?
- Does the business possess the intangible assets, including skills and capabilities, required to succeed in this market?
- Can the company attract qualified and desirable talent to support the business?

■ Is strategic advantage sustainable, and can it be monetized?

■ What would be the exit strategy, and how attractive would the business be to an acquirer such as a private equity firm?

Optimizing profit is generally linked in lock step with satisfying customers in some systemic way. Of the research that organizations may conduct as a preface to strategic planning, perhaps the most important involves understanding customer perceptions and needs.

The field of ethnography deals with discovering undiscovered needs; problems that customers are not able to articulate. Alex Lee, President of OXO International, marketer of Good Grips products, said, "When evaluating a concept for a new measuring cup, we noticed that users were repeatedly bending down to read the measurements on the side, adding or subtracting liquid, then bending down again to check the measurement. They never identified this as an inconvenience; they accepted it as part of the measurement process."

As a result of this insight, OXO designed an Angled Measuring Cup which makes it possible for the consumer to view the measurement from above."[16] Note that OXO is not a big branded company with a complex product or big market research budget. They were just highly intentional in their method for designing products based on customer needs.

I was once working a conference and had a chance to have lunch with Tom Kelley, the General Manager of IDEO, the nation's premier design firm that developed the first Palm device, Apple mouse and hundreds of leading consumer products. Tom's brother David, the founder of IDEO, is known as perhaps the world's most important designer. In David's words, his most important achievement was a "milestone in aviation history, the 747 Lavatory Occupied Sign."[17]

Tom was working with Disneyland at the time I met him and he told me that his engagement centered on improving customer experiences because Disney had concluded that their customers were already spending all they could afford in the park. That is brand power!

Kelley and his cohorts at IDEO are leaders within the field of ethnography, which could also be described as reverse engineering a product based on latent needs. As David Kelley says, "Fish don't know when they are wet."

IDEO became well known after ABC's Ted Koppel did a segment on the company on "Nightline," issuing a challenge of designing a new product in a week. The producers selected the concept of developing a new and improved grocery shopping cart (including a removable shopping basket). IDEO came through with flying colors, producing a highly functional prototype that they unveiled on the air one week later. But the real story was the road that IDEO took to create a better mouse trap.

IDEO's "Deep Dive" methodology has five steps:

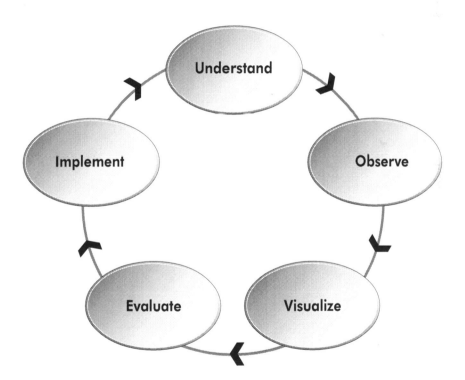

On one project, IDEO researchers observed kids using toothbrushes, and came to realize that young children held their brushes in a fist, because their hands were too small to grasp the toothbrushes that were made for them. They then created a fatter design for Oral B to meet this consumer need, one that wouldn't have been communicated through any survey or focus group.

What Kelley refers to as "design thinking" has deep implications for marketers who are looking for features and benefits that create differentiation for their brand. Even in smaller companies with limited budgets, scientific approaches can be applied to understanding customer's latent needs.

> *Every company should have a methodology for doing a deep dive into customer experiences to diagnose how customers use products and services.*

One of the core competencies within our firm is completing customer insight studies, which can serve as a precursor to strategic planning. We often learn some amazing things. In one case, our client's Vice President of Sales swore that their sales people called on every customer quarterly, only to find out during our survey process that a third of the customers couldn't name their sales rep at all.

Another method for gaining customer insights is through Customer Advisory Boards (whenever practical). My experience has been that having several customers in the same room produces a raw energy, a synergistic ability to conjure up improvements to products and services that one might not hear when conducting a more traditional individual interview. It is amazing what insights can be gleaned from having a small panel of customers provide input, answering questions such as:

- What are the criteria you use for selecting vendors?
- What are the fundamental problems you face in your role?
- How are you evaluated?
- What technologies do you see emerging that can break down the barriers between vendors and suppliers?
- How will the face of the industry change in the next few years, and how can our company be in a position to succeed?

Customer Advisory Boards (generally facilitated by a professional) are also self-fulfilling. Members of the Board will often be early adopters of the ideas generated in a panel and will take a personal interest in seeing such initiatives succeed.

Chapter 5 Review

⁕ Strategic planning is a process with inputs and outputs.

⁕ Assumptions should be made only on validated data.

⁕ A company's goals, key performance indicators, and performance management should be a derivative of the strategy.

⁕ A critical component in determining of the value proposition is the reverse engineering of products to meet customers' latent needs.

Chapter

6

Profit, Growth and other Strategic Choices

"Ability may get you to the top, but it takes character to keep you there."

— JOHN WOODEN

The formulation of strategy challenges an organization to resolve several vital questions within the context of its mission. The mission may be geared toward profit, or other pursuits such as preservation of the environment or social enterprise.

The most pivotal questions generally deal with balancing the tension between profitability and growth in such a way that optimizes the long term value of the company. With the exception of ultra high growth start ups (such as in the technology sector), growth without profit does not yield an adequate market valuation or salable asset. Lower growth trajectories may be sought after by more mature companies in markets that offer low volume but higher margins.

> One has to earn the right to grow by sustaining a profit in order to attract new capital, whether it is from banks or investors.

When businesses are offered for sale, private equity firms and investment bankers seek to identify "value drivers," the key defining elements of a business that will ensure its sustainability. To maximize such value, companies must demonstrate that they have identified and implemented a driving strategy that is an enabler to long term revenue and profitability growth. There may be other value drivers such as diversification, management depth, intellectual capital, etc.

It has been fascinating to witness this tension play out in Silicon Valley, where there has been a battle between the culture of ideas vs. the culture of money, often illustrated in ads where Apple openly mocks Microsoft, perceived as the money hungry stodgy competitor only interested in profit.[18]

In this chapter we will explore strategies that companies may employ to realize sustainable strategic advantage that strikes a balance between profit and growth.

Market Penetration

Market penetration is a strategy whereby a company or firm expands within its existing core competency. The deepening of core competencies is both an offensive and defensive strategy. Clearly, growing within existing market boundaries presents the lowest risk. Expanding share of wallet with existing customers is cheaper than acquiring new ones. As the marketer penetrates deeper, the emphasis is on getting existing customers to buy all products and services offered and to maintain high customer loyalty.

Expansion within an existing market space is often a function of continuous improvement (sometimes referred to as renovation).[19] The existing offering is the one that competitors are most likely to copy. While economies of scale and efficiencies gained through tribal knowledge reduce costs, price pressure makes acceptable margins difficult to maintain. In order to maximize selling opportunities with existing customers, the marketer must look for cross selling opportunities or up-selling of higher priced goods.

Business Transformation and Expansion

Business transformation is the art of taking an existing competency and applying it to new markets in order to satisfy differing customer needs. Expansion of an existing business if often referred to as "horizontal integration" or economies of scope. The marketer should seek out markets where they can realize a clear margin advantage (10% or more). To identify new market segments without a differentiating strategy or cost advantage will only attract new competitors to the market space and dilute margins.

While presenting slightly higher risk than a penetration strategy, expansion offers the opportunity to leverage existing capacity and marketing infrastructure. Based on a consumer's experience with a brand, he is more willing to accept the value proposition in a parallel market where he believes that attributes such as quality or service are likely to be similar. Canon initially realized a core competency in camera optics, one it leveraged to expand into printers, copiers and medical electronics.[20]

It is important to recognize that the concept of the geographic market is shifting in dramatic fashion. Globalization and borderless societies have created regional economies that are no longer defined solely in nationalistic terms. Consider the emergence of Ireland as the "e-hub" of Europe. Ireland is an autonomous state of a size that it could build infrastructure to attract entire industries and thus has become a remerging economic force. Similar region states are likely to emerge.[21]

China is more an economy than a national state and offers unique opportunity as a new economic landscape. Lack of government oversight in the protection of intellectual capital requires the marketer to have particular understanding of how to navigate within such an environment.

Divide and Conquer

Companies divide and conquer when they redefine their frame of reference and identity within the markets they serve. Generally such companies apply some type of innovation to fulfill an unmet need. To address a white space is potentially the most lucrative and highest risk strategy set.

Consider Shutterfly, a company that doubled in size between 2005 and 2007 when it generated 7 million orders.[22] Shutterfly challenged the paradigm about how photographs are stored, manipulated and printed. While many Internet and social networking sites rely on banner advertising for revenue, Shutterfly found a direct to consumer delivery model and leveraged technology to allow consumers access to new services (print on demand picture books for example). With the advent of higher resolution, less expensive cameras, the face of photography has been changed forever.

There is a "learning cost" of establishing a new business as there is a time lag involved in building intellectual capital and tribal knowledge. In the case of an existing company establishing new businesses, the startup has limitations in leveraging the parent's core competencies. There may be additional investment required in people, and equipment. In fact it is often advantageous to seek out new talent who bring fresh perspective to the new business or may have experience that an internal team may not possess. There is also an opportunity cost of diluting the core businesses' talent pool when key personnel are extracted and diverted to a new venture.

Marketers are often drawn to high growth segments, and fail to focus on those where they can truly realize advantage. In *How the Mighty Fall* (the sequel to *Good to Great*), Jim Collins points out that many of the Good to Great companies failed because they ventured into new businesses that were too far afield from their core. Caveat Emptor!

Market Saturation

A saturation strategy is deployed when the marketer defines a narrow market space and aggressively markets within it. In our definition, saturation differs from penetration in that the seller may have a low market share but may saturate an area or segment within it (a company could have a 10% share nationally but have 70% of the share in Tennessee). Market saturation is often optimal for creating efficiency in marketing and distribution. Market leadership risk is low, but economic risk is high in a tight geographic area in the event there may be a natural disaster or regional economic calamity. Such has been the case in regions such as Michigan and Ohio where there was an over-reliance on the automobile industry as the driving economic force. Other businesses concentrated in those markets are feeling the pain of rampant unemployment.

Walmart routinely uses a saturation strategy when opening a new geographic market. Generally, a distribution center is built before the stores that it will supply. Then a block of stores are opened within a month or year, in a shock an awe attack of the market. Starbucks has entered entire markets practically overnight, often opening stores within a few city blocks of one another and gaining immediate marketing traction.

Vertical Integration

A vertical integration is created when an entity owns several rungs within the value chain such as a retailer owning a manufacturer. A company may purchase upstream suppliers (backward integration) or downstream buyers (forward integration).[23] Such business combinations can offer significant advantages in terms of efficiencies, cost savings and cycle times.

Vertical integration fell out of favor in the '90s as management gurus expounded on the virtues of core competencies and defraying investment in capital intense businesses. Vertical integration is making a comeback. Today's complex business and information systems offer a new set of challenges that require more seamless integration and just-in-time readiness. In the case of manufacturing businesses, better management of information allows for reduced inventories, more efficient transportation, faster cycle times and lower labor costs.

In the beverage sector, PepsiCo. and Coca-Cola shed their bottling operations in the '90s only to buy them back a decade later in an effort to control the distribution channel. In 2009–2010, Boeing purchased supplier Vought to control manufacturing standards, and Nucor purchased SHV North America to gain access to raw materials.[24]

Given the higher capital investment required, integration is often a barrier to entry, reducing the number of suppliers in a space (therefore reducing price competition). Vertical integration can be harmful to customer-vendor relationships if customers feel threatened that their supplier is competing with them. For example, if Nike is selling merchandise to Dick's Sporting Goods and also to a Niketown (vertical integration), there can be a perception that Niketown may gets exclusive merchandise or more rapid delivery.

Double and Triple Line Strategies

Companies often seek a deeper purpose than profit alone, and social and environmental bottom lines can be a vital factor in the quest for differentiation (covered in depth in Chapter 8). Corporate strategies can also be inward facing. In his book "True to our Roots", Paul Dolan describes how he created a model for sustainable businesses (as President of Fezter Vineyards) in an effort to preserve the environment, serve the community and provide a positive work experience for their employees. Sustainability was the driving force of the mission, and core business strategy. He writes:

> "On a September morning in 1987, my entire way of thinking began to change. Before that morning, I had only read about the impact of synthetic chemicals on the microbiological richness of the vineyard earth. On comparing the lush, sweet flavors of a row of organic grapes with the bland, less expressive flavors of the conventional pesticides, herbicides and fungicides, I was amazed by the dramatic difference between the two.
>
> At that moment, I could see that the continued use of chemicals at nearly every step of the grape-growing process would diminish the quality of future vintages, and surly affect the long-term market position of the winery. It was clear to me that Fetzer Vineyards and all other wineries were risking their economic futures by placing themselves in an un-sustainable position. I realized I must take action."

Dolan and his team converted the sustainable initiative into the driving force of the winery:

> "I wanted Fetzer's vineyard workers, production people, salespeople and everyone else in the company, including me, to see themselves as part of a team with a higher purpose. People want the hours and days and years they put into their work to amount to something more than a corporate bottom line. It

doesn't have to be idealistic; it just has to have per-sonal value to them. I had to find a higher purpose that would engage everyone in the organization in a compelling way. I knew we had to come at it from the perspective of being part of a larger system, and I knew it would take exploration and discovery. I wanted our purpose to combine growth and profitability while making a difference in the world, and I needed to get complete alignment on that purpose with Fetzer's parent company (Brown-Forman).

Mergers and Acquisitions

As entire books are written on this single subject, we will merely suggest that Mergers and Acquisitions (as well as Strategic Alliances) are a method for achieving any of the strategies listed above. It is often cheaper to acquire an operating entity in a white space (as an example) than to build one from scratch. As companies grow, they seek to diversify their portfolios to reduce business risk.

It has become fairly well understood that more than half of acquisitions will not fulfill their desired objectives. One of the reasons that mergers fail so often (about 64% of the time), is that organizations fail to create the appropriate structure to support the execution of the strategy.[25] As evidenced by the massive failure of the AOL/Time Warner merger, melding the culture of an established entertainment powerhouse, with an Internet company did not yield a synergistic offering.

Often boards and executives pursue such combinations for their own ego and edification. Once there is momentum behind a merger, they are hard to stop, even if the fundamentals change.

As a general rule, acquisitions are much more likely to succeed when they are formed with the intent of growing revenue in some synergistic fashion. Acquisitions based solely on economies of scale and reduction of costs often create large, stodgy companies that lose sight of customer needs along the way.

❖   ❖   ❖

Over the course of the life of a company, the organization may bridge several strategies. McDonald's initial competencies were convenience and consistency, but as result of hyper-competition the company established price leadership in the form of a dollar menu (low cost leadership as a strategy is covered in Chapter 7). To fight off competition from Starbucks, the company has launched a counter offensive in the form of McCafe gourmet coffees (business transformation).

Over the last decade, Mickey D's has acquired stakes in Chipotle Mexican Grill, Donatos Pizza and Boston Market (somewhere between expansion and divide and conquer). McDonalds has beaten the odds, as less than 10% of mature companies are able to regain momentum once their growth begins to slow.[26] It is very hard for entrepreneurs to hit it out of the park twice.

❖   ❖   ❖

Utilization of multiple strategies is important in the quest for sustainability.

Chapter 6 Review

Companies may employ several concurrent strategies to achieve strategic advantage:

- Market Penetration

- Business Expansion

- Market Saturation

- Double and Triple Bottom Line

- Vertical Integration

- Strategic Alliances

- Mergers and Acquisitions

- Low Cost Leadership

Chapter

7

The Secret Sauce: Business Discipline and Value Proposition

"There are those who look at things the way they are and ask why — I dream of things that never were, and ask why not."

— ROBERT KENNEDY

One of the most revered books about strategy is *The Discipline of Market Leaders* by Michael Treacy and Fred Wiersema. The book (first published in 1997) was based on a study of 80 companies who had achieved market leadership. Treacy and Weirsema created three descriptors for how the organizations created value:

One group viewed product performance or uniqueness as the pivotal component of value (3M, Nike). A second group invested heavily in personalized service to meet customers' individual needs. These companies were exceptional at building customer relationships (Nordstrom, Lexus). The third group focused on operational excellence through a combination of low prices and dependability (Fed Ex, Hertz, McDonald's).

Treacy and Weirsema's premise was that companies should invest their resources in dominating within one discipline instead of diluting their offering by attempting to dominate all three. They also made the assertion that the underlying management and business structure should be built to support the focused discipline:

Product Innovation (Best Product)	Customer Intimacy (Best Solution)	Operational Excellence (Best Cost)
▪ Focus on research and development and market development.	▪ Focus on advisory services and relationship management.	▪ Focus on product supply, expedient service, demand management

It is important to note the distinction between an operationally excellent company and one that is the low-cost operator. McDonald's is a company that exhibits remarkable consistency. If you go into a McDonald's in Tampa or one in San Diego, you will be served a Big Mac with two all beef patties, special sauce, lettuce, cheese, pickles, onions on a sesame seed bun, cooked exactly to the same temperature. The bathrooms will be relatively clean. You never, ever have to be concerned with there being any deviation from the standard.

You may not like the taste of a McDonald's burger, but it is always the same. After a drive-thru customer has been waiting past the allotted time, alarms go off to signify that the speed of service is outside the standard. In McDonald's case, the value proposition is shaped by a trade-off of food quality for speed and consistency.

While Walmart is viewed by many as a villainous company who ruthlessly drains suppliers and pays low wages, the story of the company's rise to prominence as a low-cost leader is truly remarkable and serves as a rich learning ground for smaller companies.

On the heels of its growth as a mass market discounter, Walmart entered the grocery business in 1990, in a saturated market populated by Safeway, Albertsons and Kroger who had been selling groceries since 1883.[27] In the decade that followed, Walmart opened a staggering 888 supercenters, seven per month for 120 months in a row.[28] By 2000, Walmart had become the largest grocer in the US. Between the year 2000 and 2006, Walmart added another 1000 Supercenters. The average US household spends over $2,000 per year at Walmart. From toys to health and beauty aids, Walmart is the category killer in just about every segment it chooses to dominate.

Walmart is the poster child for being a low-cost operator because being efficient is interwoven into its DNA. The entire business culture is driven by a simple premise: to serve their customers, they must reduce costs in every way imaginable, which has been a source of extraordinary innovation.

Walmart decided early that the only way that they could be the cheapest was to control distribution. While Kmart was purchasing dry groceries from wholesalers, Walmart was building a national web of distribution centers. Only after a distribution center was built in a region would a grouping of stores be built around it, creating scale quickly (market saturation model).

These advantages created a spread of several percentage points, greater than the net profit of the very competitors Walmart was stealing share from. Market saturation is also the approach employed by Starbucks, which locked up superior locations in several pockets at a time in urban areas.

Walmart's vendor replenishment program (sometimes called co-managed inventory) was a ground breaking innovation. Vendors defray the costs of managing store and warehouse inventories, as well as taking on the burden of category management. "Category Captains" track the performance of products and make the necessary adjustments to assortment, price, placement, promotion, etc.

Walmart is a data driven company, operating with the world's largest private computer system. Through the company's innovative Retail Link system, suppliers have real time access to sales information by store, allowing them to make decisions on manufacturing, distribution, and promotion.

Walmart works with suppliers to take cost out of the system, collaborating on everything from pack sizes to transportation (often picking up merchandise with its enormous US fleet). Walmart was among the first to have suppliers drop ship pallets directly to its stores, reducing its handling costs.

ARCO is the low-cost oil producer. ARCO developed its own oil distribution system and only produces the grade needed to sell to its am-pm stores, which regularly undercut competitors by 10 cents or more (gasoline is a product where consumers pay close attention to prices).

Southwest Airlines, the clear low-cost airline, has been constructed from the ground up for efficiency, using only 737s, offering no business class or food and flying out of Chicago's Midway, Oakland, Burbank and Long Island airports. During the post 9/11 era, Southwest Airlines has been under fierce attack from every major airline (including Delta, United and Continental) who have attempted to copy their low-cost, short route strategy. They all have failed.

The brilliance of Southwest's strategy is in simplicity which translates beautifully into a value proposition that the consumer clearly understands. Southwest promises the consumer nothing, other than to get from point A to point B on time, at the lowest possible cost.

Southwest consistently out executes their competitors on that promise. In 2008, Southwest had an on time percentage of 81% compared to 72% for United.[29] They mishandled 4.13 per thousand bags compared to United's 7.52. Southwest fielded only one-fifth as many complaints with the US Department of Transportation.

United has hubs in San Francisco (which has an average on-time percentage of 58%) and Chicago (56%), amongst the worst performing airports in the country. If you were the airline's strategist and on-time percentage were a critical success factor, you would not locate a hub in those cities.

Yet it is United that claims in its advertising to offer "The Friendly Skies" with imagery of clouds and a peaceful travel experience. Their messaging makes a promise that they regularly fail to deliver.

> *This illustrates that it is often not the brilliance of the strategy (you could draw Southwest's on a napkin), but the execution of it that creates competitive advantage. The other carriers are not built from the ground up to support low-cost leadership.*

So what can small and midsized companies learn from the likes of Walmart, ARCO and Southwest? To be the low-cost operator typically requires scale (or some type of technological advantage which generally requires scale to maintain) and a complete unfettered, commitment to systematically cutting costs. The low-cost leader must establish an entire supply chain or service model that enables that end. To compete against these companies on price is a zero sum game if your business is low volume.

However, companies can compete on value. Value is about managing a series of compromises. Costco's CEO said, "Customers shop with us for value. They don't shop with us for cheap prices on cheap merchandise. They expect us to deliver value on quality."[30]

Simply put, the value proposition is the perceived value of the promises you make, and an organization's ability to deliver against those promises. Our client, Internet Services West, an Internet services provider in Los Angeles, runs two "data centers" protected against fire, water hazard, power outages and earthquakes. The facilities are almost indestructible and are supported by IS West's independent generators (cleverly nicknamed Edison and Watson). The IS West value proposition comes down to one simple promise; we don't go down. The company's tag line reinforces that commitment: "Non-Stop Internet, Non-Stop Support, Non-Stop People."

Counter to being low-cost operators, even high-end establishments can be operationally excellent, and they often have to be. For example, consider the speaker who described the setup for his talk at the Four Seasons Resort Aviara in Carlsbad, California. As he prepared for his speech, he approached the podium only to look down and see the catering staff preparing the room with tables and chairs, classroom style.[31]

Three men proceeded row by row with pieces of string to set up every glass in the room to insure that were perfectly aligned in a matrix. High end hotels must be operationally excellent because their customers have an expectation that service be consistent.

I once did a retreat at Bacara Resort, a tony resort in Santa Barbara, California, where an ocean view room is $1,000 per night and up. During my set up for the retreat, the catering staff seemed completely unprepared. I had to ask four different people to get an extension cord. Because Bacara is an upper-end property, my expectations for excellence were heightened and I was more likely to be disappointed.

I have a client who loves staying at the Four Seasons because he knows his individual preferences (such as staying on the ground floor) are kept in a customer profile. Each time he checks into a Four Seasons property, the staff adheres to his personal preferences, the definition of customer intimacy.

Whenever I ask groups of CEOs which of the three disciplines describes their company best, customer intimacy always wins by a landslide.

Customer Relationship Management has taken on an ugly tone over the last few years as organizations have become so consumed with integrating complex CRM systems that they have often missed the entire point of CRM (or One-to-One Marketing as it was once known).

> *Every company thinks they are close to their customers. Yet, most do not believe they can get away with passing on price increases and are in a fire fight for business every day, which would suggest that their customer relationships are not as strong as they think they are.*

The premise of the concept is that customer's individual needs should be met, and investment in meeting needs should be based on the lifetime value of the customer. That is, the more valuable the customer, the more services they should receive.

The other principle of CRM that is often lost in translation is that you always take better care of a customer you already have, than ones that you would have to pay for to acquire (the retention cost of an existing customer is generally relatively low).

Often new customers are provided with special discounts as incentives to change suppliers. The problem is that the customer motivated by such discounts has the loyalty of a cat and will change suppliers again to take advantage of yet another discount. Cell phone carriers routinely employ this tactic which is why they have such poor customer loyalty.

I am amazed that I often come across salespeople who are resistant to sharing information about their customers with their own organization. They operate under the faulty assumption that sharing information about customer needs and preferences diminishes their value, and that they could be put out to pasture. This is a self limiting belief in an age when CRM systems are integrated with supply chain systems and other processes that can enrich the customer experience. It is downright damaging in the case of a customer intimate company, because to serve a customer at a high standard requires teamwork and sharing of information.

Execution of a customer intimate model requires a mindset where satisfying customers comes before short term profit. Nordstrom must stock ample inventory in every size in order to ensure that a customer never experiences an out of stock, even though the inventory carrying costs are higher to do so. Walmart employs the opposite strategy, carrying the bare minimum of a given item).

As noted earlier, it was Intel founder Geoffrey Moore, who proclaimed that processing speed would double every 18 months while prices remained constant or decline. Imagine the pressure to produce such results! At Intel, the R&D approach is truly unique.

Whenever Intel designs a new generation of chip, competing teams submit their product design. Then, management selects the best design, and the losing team is folded into the winning team to complete the project, leveraging selected features of the losing design to improve the winning one. Only a workplace culture, built to support innovation could thrive on such internal competition and constant reorganization of staff. People who work at Intel know that to succeed in that environment, they need to accept that they could have a new manager every six months.

> In the case of product innovators, the entire structure
> of the corporation is established with innovation and
> organizational agility in mind — from the R&D budget to
> the recruiting infrastructure and office design.

Regardless of if a company is operationally excellent, customer intimate or a product/service innovator, it must be constructed from the ground up to support its business discipline.

The operating environment has changed dramatically since *The Discipline of Market Leaders* was published (in 1997):

- Globalization has brought about heightened expectations on the part of customers who now have access to an endless array of suppliers from which to choose.
- Technological advances have brought about automation of core business processes (such as customer relationship management) which have reduced costs and allowed greater productivity.

- As manufacturing has been off-shored and out-sourced, the most valued segments of the value chain have shifted from making the products to engineering, marketing, and selling them.
- Hyper-competition has brought tremendous price pressure and an environment where customers are not accepting of price increases.
- Value creation has shifted from developing new products to developing the unique services that deliver such products (service innovation).

Consider the value proposition of Dell Computers. Dell revolutionized the delivery mechanism for PC's. During the first generation of personal computing, the distribution model was three tiered (manufacturer- retailer-small business/consumer).

By moving to a consumer direct model, Dell cut out the unnecessary middleman and reduced the average number of days a computer sat in inventory. Because of the dynamics of Moore's Law (technology performance will double every 12–18 months while prices decline) , a PC that sat in a Best Buy store for 14 days was on average 4% less functional than a similar Dell product that they could offer at lesser price. In other words, technology was moving so fast, a PC sold in a retail store was almost obsolete by the time a consumer brought it home. Dell's service model slaughtered the likes of IBM, Hewlett Packard, Compaq and Gateway.

Michael Dell's book *Dell on Dell* was considered a manifesto on customer relationship management (CRM). Dell was a pioneer in implementing CRM, and its platform is certainly customer intimate. If you call Dell on the phone, the agent is aware of every transaction you have completed with Dell.

But Dell's greatest strength is the company's operational excellence. Dell is remarkably consistent with their accuracy and on-time delivery. They routinely assemble a mass customized computer and ship it within 2–3 days.

While operationally excellent, Dell is an example of a company that has constructed a value proposition that combines value, operational excellence, and customer intimacy, delivered in a revolutionary service model. Dell has proven that these three business disciplines are not in conflict and pursuing a multi-pronged value proposition can improve the customer experience.

However, strategy in the hyper-competitive marketplace comes down to managing contradictions and prioritizing what services can be offered at a price the customers will pay. The authors of *Extreme Toyota* point out the six compromises faced by chief engineer Ichro Suzuki in developing the LS 400:[32]

- Outstanding high-speed control and stability/excellent riding comfort
- Fast and smooth ride/outstanding fuel efficiency
- Elegant styling/outstanding aerodynamic performance
- Outstanding high-speed stability/excellent air resistance
- Warm ambiance/functional cabin

It is contradictory to offer a car that is fast, and gets great fuel efficiency (at least it has been that way with fuel burning engines, a paradigm that could change).

As the concept of value has taken on many dimensions and variables, customers' expectations are shifting. To understand which customer features and benefits warrant investment, organizations need to be completely consumed with assessing customer needs and quantifying which features they are willing to pay a premium for.

⁘ ⁘ ⁘

Do you have a systematic approach for assessing customer needs?

Chapter 7 Review

- Companies can be defined by the method by which their customers derive value: operational excellence, customer intimacy and product/service innovation.

- Companies must be built from the ground up to support their business discipline.

- Today's hypercompetitive business climate promotes competency in all three disciplines.

- Companies must set expectations based on the service level that is achievable within their business discipline.

Chapter

8

The Decision:
Scarcity or Abundance

*"What is a cynic? A man who knows the price
of everything and the value of nothing."*

— OSCAR WILDE

Go into any suburban Walmart on any weekend and the parking lot will include a representation of Mercedes Benz and BMWs. Twenty two-percent of Walmart shoppers have household incomes of $85,000 or more.[33] Board a Southwest flight, and you may be sitting next to a passenger wearing a Rolex watch.

This bizarre phenomenon is known as "treasure hunting." Consumers are trading down on some goods so that they can afford luxury goods such as Coach and Rolex. In the acquisition of goods and services, the consumer's purchase triggers alternate between quality, service, and price. It is as if a wedge has been driven into the traditional pricing model.

> *The transparency of markets and the resulting hyper-competition have forced marketers to make a critical choice: will we be the low-cost operator, or smother the customer with service? Do we pursue a strategy of scarcity, or one of abundance?*

Void of differentiation, any product is purely a commodity. Only those organizations that can create the infrastructure, sourcing relationships, variable costs and scale, can be the low-cost leaders. It requires a mindset of scarcity (working with less).

When afforded the privilege of visiting Walmart's corporate office in Bentonville, Arkansas, one is struck by the minimalist nature of their building, office decor and meeting rooms. It is as if Walmart makes a statement with everyone associated with them that they expect to be frugal in everything they do. One supplier tells a story of calling on a purchasing Vice President at Walmart whose office décor was lawn furniture, obviously provided by vendors.

Thus Walmart's mojo is more than hammering suppliers on cost and selling cheaply; it is an entire scarcity mindset of how can we do more with less? While Walmart is a B2C company, their suppliers, some of which are smaller companies, are B2B to some degree must adopt a scarcity mentality if they want to play in Walmart's massive sandbox.

Low-cost operators often focus on offering fewer products for which they have more purchasing power. Aldi, the German based grocery operator, is posing a threat to Walmart in the eastern US. The average Aldi store is 15,000 square feet and offers only 700 SKUs (stock-keeping units) compared to the 25,000 items carried by a conventional supermarket.[34]

By limiting their offering, Aldi has reduced carrying costs and can be extraordinarily efficient by carrying few high velocity items and shipping them into the store by the pallet (minimizing labor).

There are inherent problems in being the low-cost operator:

- Low-cost is typically a function of scale, and any market worth owning will typically be dominated by larger companies that have the capital to outspend smaller competitors and the patience to undercut the market.
- Only 2–3 companies in a market space can create enough scale to sustain a profit on little margin.
- When margins are low, risk is high. One or two quarters of soft sales or unforeseen calamity can put the low-cost operator out of business.
- Lower cost segments have a lower barrier to entry.

Outsourcing has created new opportunities for competitors to create virtual scale. A smaller supplier with an idea can have a design firm design it, an engineering firm engineer it, and an offshore production facility build it, without even an office space.

While these competitors may not have the resources to fend off larger companies, some will certainly be willing to work on little or no margin as a point of entry in an effort to buy business.

When attacked by a low-cost operator, the incumbent must ask themselves if the rival provides a substantial threat, and if customers are likely to switch based on the potential savings. The response should not be to merely match prices but to look for differentiating benefits.

There is also an experiential element to treasure hunting. Companies such as Costco and Trader Joe's are masters at creating the treasure hunt. By moving displays regularly, and providing numerous seasonal and off-beat offerings, they create the sense that every trip to the store provides a unique new experience, where brand new treasures may be discovered at a great price.

Office Max recently ran a promotion where any shopper could get 15% off all of the product they could fit inside a paper bag that Office Max included as a Sunday newspaper insert. In lieu of just putting product on sale, they created an adventure.

The department store business provides a telling example of the struggle to price in the middle. While Nordstrom and Walmart continue to flourish, Montgomery Ward's, Kmart, Sears, Mervyn's and numerous other mid-priced chains are closed, bankrupt or otherwise doomed. The merger of Sears and Kmart was like two guys who didn't know how to swim holding onto one another in the deep end.

Only Target, who has differentiated through clever advertising and merchandising, has appealed to the core demographic: middle class housewives (note that Target is a discounter but priced higher than Walmart). While Target's rise is impressive, Walmart eclipses Target's total sales by March of each year.

The mid-priced offer is confusing to today's consumer because they don't know what to make of it. The consumer cannot reconcile if the supplier is providing superior quality and service, or if they are positioned as low price.

The middle is invariably the most crowded of any market segment. Consider the positioning of popular restaurant chains during the economic downturn in 2008–2009. The following table illustrates operating margins for leading national chains in March 2009, shortly after Bennigan's and Steak and Ale filed for Chapter 7 liquidation:[35]

White Table Cloth	• Ruth's Chris—6.0% • Morton's—2.7%
Casual Specialty	• Cheesecake Factory—5.6% • Olive Garden/Red Lobster—8.6%
Casual	• Bennigan's, Steak and Ale—Chapter 7 • Ruby Tuesday's—4.8%
Fast Casual	• Panera—8.9% • Corner Bakery/Chili's—6.1%
Fast	• McDonalds—26.7% • YUM (KFC, TB, PH)—12.4%

Even at a time when consumer confidence and access to discretionary income were low, white table cloth restaurants Ruth Chris and Morton's were able to maintain a minimal operating profit. The Cheesecake Factory, Olive Garden and Red Lobster, themed restaurants with a higher price point and differentiated menu, were able to cut 6–8%. Fast casual Panera and the operator of Corner Bakery, offering a differentiated fresher alternative to fast foods, maintained operating margin of 6–9% compared to an astonishing 27% for McDonald's.

The problem with being the low-cost operator is that others in this space are constantly pressuring margins with lower price points and seeking out opportunities to buy market share.

When scale can be achieved, the bottom end can make money on purchasing power and operating efficiencies. Much like the department store industry, mid-priced restaurants' margins have deeply eroded.

By 2004, Southwest Airline's costs were 6.2 cents per available seat mile compared to 8 cents for other carriers.[36] Jet Blue entered the market at 4.7 cents, providing a new level of cost cutting to the market and creating a greater threat to Southwest than United's, Delta's or Continental's failed attempts to offer a low-cost alternative. At the bottom, prices are constantly under pressure.

Over the last 20 years, many US manufacturers have implemented lean manufacturing in order to maintain momentum toward lower costs. To be lean, an organization must continuously be faster, smarter, better, and, yes, cheaper.

The economics of pricing on the high end is typically more lucrative as there is less competition and less risk. When products are scarce, we expect to pay more for them. What we want most is what we can't have.

Exclusive distribution arrangements protect the pricing of a product or service. Retailers such as Trader Joe's and GNC sign exclusive distribution agreements to protect their control brands (brands that they control through partnerships but they do not own). Appliance manufacturers try to promote exclusivity by offering a refrigerator at one retailer with one SKU (stock-keeping unit) and model number, and practically the same model at another retailer under a different model number, betting that most consumers won't be able to tell the difference.

The days of cost-plus pricing (adding a fixed percent to the cost to arrive at a price) are over. Pricing is purely a function of supply and demand. Have you ever noticed that the price of gasoline goes up much faster than it goes down? That is because once consumers are accustomed to paying a price, gas marketers will lock in at a higher price point. Even if costs plummet, prices will remain higher until discounters erode the market.

Buyers instinctively understand that vendors who provide more services will be more expensive than those who offer less. They may choose an American supplier for a component that requires a fast turnaround time, and different one when cost is the purchase lever. While purchasing departments in B2B environments are certainly becoming more sophisticated and price sensitive, those companies who are able to demonstrate a strategic approach to selling and sell on the "total cost of ownership" can overcome obstacles such as auctions and request-for-quotes (RFQs) based solely on price.

Often marketers commoditize their own products through rapid discounting. The reverse is also true; those companies who have focused on seeking out white spaces are the ones who have maximized shareholder value.

As characterized in Blue Ocean Strategy, circuses were a low value activity before Cirque de Soleil, and coffee was commoditized before Starbucks brought the marketplace a new offering.[37]

The pricing wedge also promotes a mindset where those companies who wish to be differentiated must seek continuous innovation, as competitors will copy various services creating an environment in which a supplier's service bundle must continuously be expanded.

Products are commoditized, but brands are differentiated.

There is an exception to these principles. Consider the variant pricing model provided by Coca-Cola. In a white table cloth restaurant, one might pay $4 for a twelve ounce Coca-Cola. In a fast food restaurant, perhaps 99 cents for twenty ounces. In a vending machine, a dollar for twelve ounces and in a grocery store $2.19 for two liters (for those of us who are metrically challenged, that is about seventy ounces). So, in a restaurant, the consumer is paying 10 times on a cost per ounce basis than they would in a grocery store for an identical product.

This dynamic illustrates two important points:

a) The market price of a product is driven by the usage type of the consumer.

b) To establish higher margin businesses, customers may be acquired at lower price points.

It is the same strategy employed by credit card companies such as American Express (Green, Gold, and Platinum) where customers are acquired at a lower price point and then trade up to more expensive cards with more robust benefits. Low-end segments can be used as a lever to drive growth of mid and high priced offers, only if they do not dilute the value of the brand.

For example, McDonald's offers a Dollar Menu as a loss leader. When my wife takes the kids to McDonald's on the weekend, she pays $1 for a hot fudge sundae. My bratty children (only interested in what they want and not economy), always want McFlurries at $2.79. Retailers and restaurants understand the concept of blended margins, to offer the $1 hot fudge sundae and make a profit, one cannot discount the McFlurry.

Marketers do not need to have fat R&D budgets or use highly scientific methods to gain customer insights that can drive innovation as a business discipline and create price separation. Innovation comes from asking the right questions, observing behavior, and following people around, even in a B2B environment.

One of our clients used such a methodology with their largest customers. During an interview with a controller, they were told that their invoices were confusing and that it would save their office a lot of time if the invoices were structured differently. They also requested a monthly summary of invoices. Our client retooled their invoicing procedures. Imagine if you did the same with your client's purchasing department?

This may not seem like a major innovation, but in the eyes of the person cutting the checks, our client has found a solution that created separation from other suppliers in the payment queue. Who do you think gets paid first: the vendor whose invoices are easy to reconcile, or the ones that take more time? A controller may not be a key decision maker, but in the hyper-competitive marketplace, relationships must go deep and wide.

The contrast between scarcity and abundance becomes even more evident at the bottom of the business cycle. Some companies take every conceivable step to cut costs while others take a counterintuitive view and seek to build share.

During the Great Depression, Post Cereals cut back on marketing and research and development (a scarcity approach). Kellogg's, working with an abundance mindset, increased its advertising and developed a high growth brand in Rice Krispies. At the time, economist Roland Vaile did a study that revealed that companies who increased ad spending during the Depression performed better during the upturn, a study replicated by McKinsey & Company during the recession in the early '90s.[38]

Upper-end providers must protect their value proposition even when times are tough. Consider the positioning of Coach, the producer of upscale (if not pretentious) handbags. Through March of 2009, the company reported earnings over three quarters of $478 million, compared to $570 million the prior year. Gross Margins slipped from 75.6% to 72.4%. As inventory started to build, the company's cash reserves slid from $608 to $551. In July of 2008, before the recession was in full bloom, Coach's consumer research identified a need for a lower entry point for consumers, and developed "Poppy" a line of handbags at price points 20% lower than Coach's core products.[39]

Even a super luxury brand like Coach can offer a lower price alternative without corrupting the brand. Most CFOs would be envious of Coach's margin and cash position, which were built through a high margin offer. The company had the discipline to save wisely so that they could survive a significant downturn which had far reaching implications to pricing, positioning and investment.

Changing your business discipline mid-stream is confusing to the marketplace. Regardless of the business cycle, marketers must be consistent in terms of their pricing and offering so that they can be in a position to take advantage of the upturns to follow.

Chapter 8 Review

- Hyper-competition has created a "pricing wedge" in the marketplace. Customers have a "treasure hunting" mentality as they trade down on less expensive goods so that they can afford to trade up on luxury goods.

- Retailers have capitalized on the treasure hunting phenomena by creating adventures for their customers.

- Marketers need to be careful not to price in the middle as buyers cannot differentiate their offer. The purchase lever alternates between quality, service, and price.

9

Points of Differentiation

"We're not in the hamburger business,
we're in the show business."

— RAY KROC

In a world where products and services can be commoditized quickly, every marketer comes to a fork in the road. The choice is to be the low-cost operator or find points of differentiation. Here are some strategies for separating from the pack:

Using Service Innovation as a Differentiator

According to *BusinessWeek*, the companies who best monetize innovation are those who disrupt an industry service model.[40] The chart below presents revenue growth from 2004–2007 for innovation leaders in the Fortune 500:

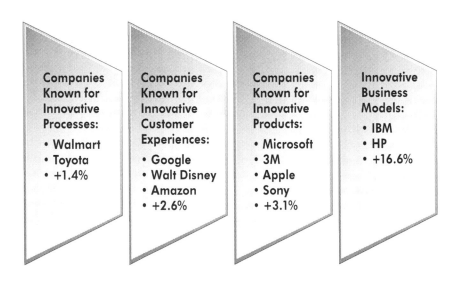

Companies Known for Innovative Processes:
- Walmart
- Toyota
- +1.4%

Companies Known for Innovative Customer Experiences:
- Google
- Walt Disney
- Amazon
- +2.6%

Companies Known for Innovative Products:
- Microsoft
- 3M
- Apple
- Sony
- +3.1%

Innovative Business Models:
- IBM
- HP
- +16.6%

I am ashamed to say that there are four iPods in my house, and two of them belong to me. While the iPod is certainly a revolutionary product, Apple took a strangle hold on the music industry not through the iPod, but by bundling the product with iTunes. While the iPod (a product innovation) is a wonderful product, it was not the first MP3 player to market.

> *Although the iPod is sexy and gets all the attention, it is iTunes (a service innovation) which reframed the delivery system for music and was the real disrupter.*

Why is iPod so cool? Because it celebrates our individuality. You can create your own custom playlist based on your individual preferences. It is like being a DJ, and DJs are cool.

Service innovations are less costly to produce than product innovations. Apple is outsourcing innovation to third party developers through distribution on the "App Store" (Salesforce is doing the same with "AppExchange").

Service innovation occurs when companies anticipate needs before customers do. Zip Car is disrupting the delivery system for auto transportation, challenging the assumption that cars are worth owning in major metropolitan markets.

Offered primarily in urban markets, Zip Cars are available at a low-cost at the time that people need them (such as college students visiting their parents out of town for an afternoon). Using "Smart Cars," Zip Car is addressing a finite niche, offering a unique product to a unique audience creating differentiation from Hertz and Avis. Enterprise, the most profitable US rental car company, also has chosen to stay out of the crowded commercial market, instead addressing the B2C market with the tag line "we will pick you up."

> *As customers expect more value in a highly saturated marketplace, it will be disruptive service innovations that will be the driver of competitive advantage in the global economy over the next decade.*

Product innovation does not always translate into competitive advantage. In a world where products are reverse engineered and replicated in sweatshops in a matter of days, products are more easily commoditized than services.

In the case of iPod, the combination of product innovation and service innovation creates a unique customer experience. The word "experience" is totally overused, but consider the value derived from customer experiences for a moment.

When you were a child and it was your birthday, your mother would go out and buy the raw ingredients and bake you a birthday cake. If you were born before 1980, it is likely that your expectation for a party was to have a few friends over, sit around the dining room table and play party games.

As the service economy of the '80s and '90s emerged, mom could go to any local grocery store with an in-house bakery and buy a ready-made cake for $10–$12.[41] Today, when a young child has a birthday, it is their expectation to have a party at a venue such as Chuck E. Cheese or at a local play gym, at a cost of $300 or more. The "experience" yields a significant price premium.

What does raw fish cost per pound in a grocery store? Let's assume $12–$14 per pound for fresh fish (product). If the grocery adds some marinade (service), they can charge a couple of dollars more. What does fish cost per pound in a Sushi restaurant? $100 per pound or more!

Certainly, the quality of the fish is superb in a sushi restaurant, but it is the experience of the chef yelling "Arigato" when you enter the Sushi bar, and slamming down sake with your friends (you know who you are) that creates at least a 500% price premium.

> From Chuck E. Cheese to Disneyland to ritzy cigar bars charging $100 for a glass of cognac, we are in the midst of an experience economy, and customers pay dearly for top drawer experiences.

Every customer touch shapes a new experience. Consider how customers are treated when they visit a service provider's office or plant. When customers enter the lobby, they are typically greeted by a receptionist and asked to sign in, and perhaps have a seat in the lobby as she summons internal staff.

A unique experience would be if the receptionist were to show the initiative to get up, move around the physical barrier, and welcome the customers with a handshake (like a salesperson would at Nordstrom). A sign may welcome the customers, or perhaps their customer support team could be waiting for them in the lobby.

Then, a customer tour might look something like this: Stations would be set up around the building with experts from your company who provide an example of what is done, by whom and why (this could just as easily be done in an insurance company or manufacturing facility). These people would be positioned as subject matter experts. Perhaps there is something interactive that the customers can sense (touch, feel, hear or taste). Maybe they could experience their own products being produced.

Finally, they are led to a conference room where the team that supports them is awaiting their arrival. The customers are asked a series of probing questions about their business issues (diagnose the pain), and how the company could innovate to meet their needs. Then a customer presentation about the performance of your products (as it relates to the customer) is made. Such a tour could take on many forms, but the opportunity is to leverage the time the customer is investing with you to create a highly differentiated experience.

Our client Southern California Graphics is a regional printer. Their offer is high-end (including print media for movies, auto manufacturers, etc.). When a client comes to Southern California Graphics, sometimes they may have to wait for modifications to be made to a "proof."

They don't wait in a conference room; they wait in a customer lounge, with a full kitchen, leather couches, flat screen television and bar. It is like being at home. Company President Tim Toomey knows they are there, and often personally comes by to say hello, hear how they are doing and make sure that his company's service is up to par. The extra touches send a message to the customer: you are like our family, and we want you to be comfortable here.

We also suggest clients conduct touch point assessments to assess if they are easy to do business with. Be a customer for a day and test your website, phone system, customer service department, help desk, accounting department, etc.

Customers are most often dissatisfied not by the product they consume, but how difficult it is to order, receive, or return.

❖ ❖ ❖

Expanding Your Bundle of Services as a Differentiator

The hardware chain Lowe's once ran a television commercial with a father and son standing in their driveway. The father beamed with pride as a Lowe's truck pulled up to deliver the family's new appliances. He boasted to his son what he had negotiated with Lowe's: not only to deliver the new appliances for free, but that they would pick up the old ones as well at no charge.

As the truck pulls away, you see the offer on the back of the truck, "free pick up with delivery." Lowe's ingeniously extended the transaction and provided a service not offered by their archrival, Home Depot. What do you think they are doing with those used washers and dryers? They are likely selling them for scrap at a profit.

In an environment where commoditization is endemic, one way to protect margins is to engage (perhaps subliminally) in a dialog about the total cost of ownership. In this case, to own the new washer and dryer, the buyer would have typically had to expend time, energy or money to dispose of the old washer and dryer.

When Dell and others began providing real time tracking of deliveries, it was a service innovation; but today, every company with a sophisticated supply chain offers the same service. It is no longer value added, it is just expected. So the service bundle has to keep changing as competitors replicate the service offering of the market leader.

The unique service bundle may include "signature" services. When checking into a Doubletree Hotel, guests are presented with warm chocolate chip cookies. You start thinking about the cookie in advance of checking in (I actually plan my day around checking in at the optimum time to enjoy the cookie). I am amused that a $200 a day purchasing decision may be influenced (perhaps subliminally) by a value added benefit that may cost 25 cents to produce.

There also needs to be a distinction made between expanding the bundle of services you provide and selling additional services. As electronic gadgetry became more popular, United Airlines cut off the current running to electrical outlets in their terminals and rented space to kiosk operators who now sell power as a service. In an interesting contrast, Southwest created free power stations complete with desks and chairs in some terminals in an effort to provide more value and an enhanced customer experiences.

Information as a Differentiator

Recently, I began a new food regimen that included protein for breakfast. I became hooked on Jamba Juice, in part because of the complete nutrition information offered in a binder within the store. I knew my exact intake in terms of calories and protein.

Several months later another juice operator, Robek's, opened three blocks from my house. As Jamba Juice is about two miles away, I was excited to have a closer alternative. On the first day Robek's opened, I went into the store to order a protein shake. When I asked to see nutritional information, I was shocked that all they could offer was a twofold brochure that did not include any of the low calorie drinks. If you are going take the time to print a nutrition guide, wouldn't you want to include the drinks that people most interested in nutrition would buy?

I left Robek's disappointed and did not return for several months. One day I was in a hurry and simply had no choice. Upon my return, Robek's had a different brochure, and I came to realize that some of their shakes were lower calorie than what I had typically purchased at Jamba Juice. Their offer from a nutritional standpoint was better; they were just doing a lousy job telling their story, and they lost my business.

Companies whose technologies enable us to manage information such as Microsoft, Apple and Intel are among the most highly valued in our economy. Companies who best position their information have a strategic advantage.

Providing relevant and timely information is a case where reverse engineering is powerful. Providers must always put themselves in the shoes of the customer. I recently took advantage of low interest rates and refinanced my home. The representative working my loan sent me a release that he needed signed and returned immediately so that we would close on time. There was no fax number or email on the form. I, the customer, now had to take the extra step to look up the information.

Every organization should take the time to dive deeper into the transactional requirements of their process and take out every possible redundant or inefficient step. It is not only better for the customer, it saves time for the provider as well. Every company should query customers on what information they could instantly need without having to ask you for it.

Providing better and more relevant information than competitors is a big opportunity for professional services firms who can position as thought leaders in their field. Being a *subject matter expert* is a critical tool in fighting off commoditization.

No industry has been more adversely affected by swings in the economy than construction. One purveyor of concrete, "The Concrete Network" has created a portal where customers can learn about how to use concrete, or find a contractor. As David Scott points out in *The New Rules of Marketing and PR,* "you are what you publish."

Many executives my age cannot tell the difference between a blog, or a forum or a wiki. Yet the Internet age brings a new set of realities, where a brand can be built or destroyed overnight based on ratings and message boards, thus all marketers need to build a cohesive Internet marketing strategy that addresses the emerging marketplace.

If a company can be a thought leader in concrete, imagine the implications for insurance brokers, CPAs and other service providers.

Use Third Party Validation as a Differentiator

Validation through a third party such as J.D. Power, ISO, UDSA, MS Certified or the Good Housekeeping Seal is a powerful differentiator.

The validation that I find most amusing is the concept of "Certified Pre-owned," a branding technique used by Lexus and other auto-makers. The provider is implying that you should pay more because they certify the product to be better than other competitive offers. In other words, they are certifying themselves.

Any provider of any good or service could do this by establishing a set of certifications, guidelines or practices, or partnering with a third party to provide such validation.

Often third-party validation is used to validate the skill sets of professionals including CPAs, attorneys and Microsoft specialists. Any firm could set up an internal certification and elevate the com-petency of people who serve customers.

❖   ❖   ❖

Emotional Attachment as a Differentiator

My wife and I were going to a charity event one New Year's Eve, and I decided to buy a new tuxedo. When approached by the depart-ment store salesman, I told him that I really liked that "white dinner jacket look." "Let's see how it looks on you," he replied.

Moments later the salesman appeared with a white dinner jacket in my size and I slipped it on. "That ... is James Bond," he said. I thought to myself, "Never in the history of man has a transaction closed so fast!" I was telling this story during a talk once and asserted that every man wants to be James Bond, and one of the women in the audience said, "And every woman wants to date James Bond!"

Had the salesman brought me two black jackets, I would have compared them on quality and price. But I would have paid any-thing for the white jacket. I wasn't buying a tuxedo, I was buying the opportunity to approach the bar and order a vodka martini, shaken, not stirred. I was James Bond.

Emotional marketing messages win over functional ones every time. Pepsi has been running the "Pepsi Challenge" in the form of a taste test since 1975.[42] Coca-Cola's highly acclaimed ads have included "I'd like to teach the world to sing; I'd like to buy the world a Coke" and "Have a Coke and a Smile" featuring Mean Joe Green. Coke has held its market share dominance for more than 100 years. In fact, the market capitalization derived by Coca-Cola for selling sugar water is truly extraordinary. They have done it by connecting to the consumer at an emotional level.

Budweiser's popular Clydesdale commercials do not even show beer or people drinking beer. The ads make an emotional appeal and try to reinforce American values.

One of my clients is a regional franchisee for GolfTec, the leading national golf instruction company. I asked him what he thought he was selling and he replied "golf lessons." I suggested he think of his offer differently.

The second best feeling in the entire world is hitting a 5 iron stiff, five feet from the pin (if I have to explain the best feeling, you are reading the wrong book). To experience that feeling on a regular basis would be invaluable to me, and I would pay dearly to attain it. If you are in golf instruction, what you are selling is the adrenalin the player feels after hitting the perfect shot. You are selling the rush. We advised that there be more imagery around the emotional appeal to the player.

I often see websites and marketing materials that list services and benefits but do not provide the reader with a reason to do business with the supplier. There has to be some type of emotional appeal with every offer. Emotional triggers can include love, fear, passion, vitality, etc. Emotional attachment is a powerful motivator. As in the MasterCard commercials, hitting a hole in one in front of your friends is "priceless."

❖   ❖   ❖

Authenticity as a Differentiator

Our client Streamline Design markets the "Old Guys Rule" brand of apparel and accessories. Old Guys Rule is a surfer brand made popular in the beach cities of Southern California and is now sold exclusively in surf shops on the East Coast, West Coast and Hawaii. It is not marketed to big box retailers and discounters which would cheapen the brand. By focusing on a niche market, Old Guys Rule has remained relevant.

The brand is in the mold of Streamline Design founder Thom Hill, a good businessman and an avid surfer. Thom will never sell out to the big boxes because it is not who he is. The brand has taken on the personality of the CEO. Old Guys Rule is not only a brand; it promotes a lifestyle. Old Guys Rule is the real deal.

❖   ❖   ❖

Simplicity as a Differentiator

This may seem like an oxymoron, but in today's world, ripe with complexity, offers that are simple are often preferred. Sometimes, customers don't want to have to think.

In Southern California, there is a regional burger chain known as "The Habit Burger Grill." The Habit serves only 16 items and the menu never changes. The chain's tag line, "There is no substitute for quality," is a primer for the chain's point of differentiation: quality served simply.

By serving a very simple menu, The Habit can control food costs and quality. Diners can expect the same consistent experience every time. In-N-Out Burger, one of the nation's fastest growing food chains, is of a similar ilk, except they serve a handful of menu items compared to McDonald's which often offers 50 or more.

Life has become so hectic that there is a fundamental shift toward simplicity (as in the case of Netbooks). Any offer that reduces confusion or the need to manage details is desired in the marketplace. Apple has done a masterful job in marketing the pure simplicity of the iPhone, leading to the phrase "there's an app for that."

◈   ◈   ◈

Customer Feedback as a Differentiator

The Internet has brought about a new phenomenon: the ability for customers to publicly rate their suppliers in real time. Trip Advisor is popular for travel, as Zagat is for restaurants.

As of this writing, Yelp has more than 4 million users, rating everything from local CPAs to bicycle shops. While the number of ratings for some of these businesses is quite limited, the concept should be a wakeup call for every CEO. Your products and services will be rated on the Internet in public view, even if you are B2B. It is only a matter of time.

The World Wide Web is also unique in that once things are posted there, they are hard to remove. Thus every company has to control their message on the Internet, before someone else controls the message for them.

eBay presents a telling example of what is in store, not only for Internet retailing, but for brick and mortar, and even service businesses. Every vendor is rated by a third party, and those ratings play heavily into the customer's purchasing decisions. eBay has also introduced PayPal as a third party currency to ensure a legitimate marketplace for buyer and seller, enabling the confidence to transact. Customer feedback can also be used as a marketing tool.

Of course, to collect positive feedback, customers have to be satisfied first. As will be described in the next chapter, customer loyalty is an important predictor.

◈   ◈   ◈

What makes your company uniquely different than every other company in the world?

Chapter 9 Review

Companies have a choice; they can either be the low-cost operator or create points of differentiation. Differentiating strategies include:

- Product Innovation
- Service Innovation
- Emotional Attachment
- Information
- Third Party Validation
- Customer Feedback
- Authenticity
- Simplicity

Chapter

10

The Changing Face of Customer Acquisition and Retention

"The world is changing very fast. Big will not beat small anymore. It will be the fast beating the slow."

— Rupert Murdoch

Peter Drucker said all management is marketing, but it is hard to believe he could have imagined the extent to which the advent of computer technologies would transform the field, practically overnight. In a climate where competition is severe, the world of sales and marketing has been turned upside down.

Diluted by the myriad of messages promoted online, traditional marketing approaches have lost their effectiveness. At the same time, computing has enabled more rigorous measurement of marketing productivity, heightening expectations of higher returns on marketing investment (ROMI).

We are in the new age of marketing, where traditional media (including newspaper) and print advertising have been replaced by new approaches including viral marketing techniques that can often be executed at low-cost on the Internet.

As the world of blogs, real simple syndication (RSS) feeds and social networking has taken shape, the marketing infrastructure needed to support current marketing efforts has evolved, requiring that organizations hire new talent with competencies that they often do not have in house. As this is not a marketing text per se, we will contain comments to value proposition and the like and less so on marketing tactics. Regardless of the marketing fads of the day, all marketing activities should be a derivative of the company's strategy and positioning.

A common problem among small and medium sized firms is a lack of a cohesive marketing strategy leading to poor targeting. Often, companies address too large a market, leaving a brand without identity, focus or meaning.

A strategic thinking mindset applied to sales and marketing ensures that:

- There is a synergistic relationship where marketing is an enabler to the sales process.
- There is a marketing strategy that allocates marketing resources to meet specific objectives.
- Research on consumer and industry trends is conducted regularly. Decisions are made based on real data.
- There are structured processes to gather and share market intelligence.
- There are systems to promote sales productivity such as sales force automation, CRM, etc.
- Salespeople are trained not only to sell effectively but to nurture the brand.

Central to the integration of sales and marketing is agreement on the company's brand identity and how various activities will be carried out to support it. If you are a customer intimate company and decide to promote premium pricing, discounting on the part of salespeople can sabotage the brand.

In a crowded space, auto manufacturers have done a masterful job of drilling home a single message on the customer needs they wish to address. If I say the word "Volvo," you say ... "safety." I say "BMW," you say... "The Ultimate Driving Machine" (performance). Honda is known for efficiency and reliability. Previous to its re-organization, GM had no identity and placed its bet on "An American Revolution," an approach that backfired as American cars were seen as subpar.

Companies often wrestle with the appropriate market scope. When expanding into new businesses, the least expensive markets to enter are always those directly adjacent to the ones that are already served.

Being dominant in a smaller market is generally more profitable than being a smaller fish in a larger market.

As a general rule, a company should achieve a significant share in its core market before attempting to infiltrate new segments.

Entering an adjacent market has less risk and improves the marketer's odds of achieving market leadership. Honda's core competency is building efficient and reliable engines. Honda has successfully extended their offering into engines in the motorcycle, marine and jet marketplace, leveraging its powerful branding in markets directly adjacent to that of automobile engines.

The Internet and urbanization of America have been the impetus to viral marketing, and new techniques that allow marketers to navigate the blitz of new media and create buzz. In the throes of the 2008 Presidential campaign, Baskin-Robbins released two new flavors: "Straight Talk Crunch" in celebration of John McCain, and "Whirl of Change" to represent Barack Obama. Baskin-Robbins' public relations staff had a field day, being interviewed repeatedly on national television and radio programs.

In April 2009, Lifelock did a co-promotion with "The Celebrity Apprentice." My wife set me up as a victim. In a produced online video, the announcer spoke of long lines of people who were claiming to be the "Real Marc Emmer," apparently the winner of The Celebrity Apprentice. The video showed numerous clips of examples, such as a guy who had a driver's license with my name and of the Emmer Tower (as opposed to Trump Tower).

Lifelock's play on identity theft yielded millions of hits within days, as people merely filled out a few fields with the names and email addresses of friends who would represent the next set of targets. The video spread like the plague and cleverly illustrated how quickly your identity can be taken from you.

The principles of Six Degrees of Separation have only been enhanced by the Internet, as people have the opportunity to instantly connect and create new connections with others. As of this writing, companies are figuring out how to integrate social networking with other Internet marketing and traditional marketing techniques. We are an application away from social networking being a legitimate mainstream marketing tool.

> *Central to successful sales and marketing is allocation of resources, managing both the retention of existing customers and the development of new ones, simultaneously.*

There are times when organizations must make conscious decisions about what investments they are willing to make to retain customers. For example, if energy costs rise quickly, and a company employs a surcharge, profits are preserved but customers may be alienated. Thus the value proposition and marketing activities tied to it are often about managing a set of tradeoffs to find the right offer delivered to the right set of customers at the right time.

Operating a dozen or more wine clubs at any time, the marketers at Adams Wine Group (our client) know to the penny what it costs to acquire and retain customers. Thus, they can make an informed decision on which customer relationships are worth nurturing.

Measuring things such as acquisition costs can be accomplished in any sales environment by merely taking the total marketing and sales costs and dividing that number by new business activity. While marketers often complain about the difficulty of measuring return on marketing investment, measuring the effectiveness of the entire sales and marketing effort is one of the more absolute metrics available to any organization.'

Over the last decade, customer relationship management (CRM) has become quite the fashionable business topic as companies have developed sophisticated technologies for managing and mining customer data. The implementation of CRM systems has become so expensive and time consuming that the very term CRM is now defined by some as a computer system in lieu of its true objective as a mindset by which customers are segmented and treated differently based on their lifetime value and/or specific needs and preferences.

At the same time, marketers have come up with all types of methodologies for measuring satisfaction in real time. I am afforded the opportunity to stay at world-class resorts where our clients hold their retreats and planning meetings. When traveling on business, I often stay at Marriott and Hyatt Hotels. They are well run operations and strong brands. If surveyed, I would give them high marks. I am satisfied.

But, I am loyal to Hilton. As a longtime member of Hilton HHonors, I believe that Hilton fulfills the promise of customer relationship management as a conduit to customer loyalty. Given a choice, I will travel as far as 15 miles out of my way to stay at a Hilton because I am treated extraordinarily well and I am rewarded for my business. I am routinely upgraded; always receive free breakfast and Internet services and access to lounges with free cocktails and the like. At Hilton, I am treated like a VIP.

Hilton's partnership with American Express is an extraordinarily lucrative loyalty program for the member and a clear differentiator over other brands. Hilton is simply willing to provide more benefits to the member. I have taken a free vacation with my family every year for the last five years (for me, a great vacation is based on the criterion that I don't have to take more than five steps from my hotel before touching sand).

Thus the additional investment made in me through Hilton's profiling of my wants and needs yields them thousands of dollars of incremental revenue every year, for the cost of some scrambled eggs and a few routers that Hilton can leverage across thousands of Hilton customers.

I was an "Executive Premier" on United Airlines when I lived in San Francisco (their West Coast hub at the time), meaning I was in the upper echelon of United customers. Upon moving to Los Angeles, the nature of my air travel changed as it was more equally divided among several carriers. I was shocked to learn that I lost all of my status with United in about a year.

Satisfaction alone is insufficient in terms of measuring the value of customer relationships. Customer loyalty is a far more accurate predictor of profitability.

It didn't matter how many miles I had logged, or was likely to earn in the future, I was sent to the back of the line with the leisure travelers who fly once or twice a year, and are unlikely to fly first class or purchase a membership to an executive lounge. United was only considering my current value (at that time) and failed to recognize my potential future value. Now I am spreading the word as a passenger that has logged hundreds of thousands of miles on their airline. United Airlines has treated me like crap. Both loyalists and dissenters are likely to share their experiences with others.

Another key tenant of CRM is The Pareto Principle (or the 80/20 rule, as it is often known) which proclaims that 20% of the customers drive 80% of the profit. It is clear that in the travel industry, business travelers are disproportionately valuable and certainly deserve the perks. While every hotel and airline offers loyalty programs, some are just fodder and some (such as Hilton) truly differentiate customers.

We have often counseled customers to consider various forms of customer management programs including loyalty programs that segment, track and reward customers who are disproportionately profitable. Say, for instance, that you sell widgets through distributors. Some of the distributors buy in larger quantities, pay on time, have less returns and demand less credits. These customers could be provided some type of VIP incentive at the end of the year based on their performance. The incentive could be monetary, or could be intangible such as guaranteed turnaround times, etc.

Find a way to treat your best customers like VIPs. This effort may be guided by a firm's business discipline. In the case of Walmart, the low-cost operator makes little effort to differentiate customers, where Nordstrom provides "personal shoppers" to its most valuable shoppers (a fact that I used to be often reminded of when receiving my wife's credit card bill).

> *Loyal customers are the most profitable because they typically do not use price as their primary purchase trigger (the converse is also true, that the least profitable customers are those that buy based on price).*

The same principles apply to service businesses. In the case of a CPA, some clients are clearly easier to do business with and have more upside than others and should receive different treatment based on their perceived lifetime value. You might also place a higher value on the types of clients who provide referrals or the ones who have done so in the past.

Customer intimate companies go further, measuring share of wallet, and understanding which customer relationships are improving and which are in decline. Among the questions that salespeople are often afraid to ask is, "What percentage of your overall xyz business do we have?" It is a relevant and appropriate question for a consultative salesperson to ask.

The search for loyalty measurements was the foundation of the book *The Ultimate Question* where Bain consultant Fred Reichheld developed the now popular "Net Promoter Score."

Reichheld and his colleagues separated customers into three types:

Promoters	Enthusiasts of a product who are likely to tell others and be advocates for your product or service.
Passives	Those who use your product, but could easily be induced by another offer or better price.
Detractors	Customers who are unhappy but are compelled in some way to purchase from a company with which they have a poor relationship.

While a myriad of questions can be used, Reichheld cites his version of the ultimate question: "How likely is it that you would recommend COMPANY to a friend or colleague?" The response to the question provides The Net Promoter Score, calculated as follows: Promotors–Detractors=NPS. Only a few best-in-class companies such as Southwest Airlines, Amazon, eBay, and Apple have Net Promoter Scores of 30% or more.

For small companies who have no competency in customer satisfaction, a natural starting point is to leverage a third party to survey customers regularly.

This approach is particularly important for professional services firms as 80% of new referrals come from people who provide a 9 or 10 answer to "The Ultimate Question." I have become consumed with customer satisfaction because the field is on the forefront of a major shift. In the past, customer satisfaction has been a function of vendors surveying their customers. The Internet is transforming the space as consumers are proactively rating providers.

As illustrated earlier, eBay has demonstrated a model where customers buy products from vendors with which they are not familiar, often based on the aggregated rating of the seller. They place tremendous weight on the score, even though they have little information by which they can validate the raters. Being a rater and reviewing other ratings has become an integral part of the trading culture on eBay.

Organizations need to be adept at measuring their performance before their customers start doing it for them. The opportunity in most firms is to use customer satisfaction to calibrate their internal processes with the needs of external stakeholders. In other words, continuous improvement occurs when you learn from customers and apply the learning to improve the way you do business (thus enabling higher scores in the future).

❖   ❖   ❖

In small and medium sized companies, many sales methodologies lack structure. Back in the day, best-in-class sales organizations such as IBM and Xerox trained new salespeople for a year or more before they came close to touching a customer. In my experience, extraordinary sales people must have some combination of the following elements to succeed:

a) The type of personality where they can connect with people and sustain long term relationships.
b) Access to tools such as ample research, case studies, marketing collateral and CRM.
c) A competitive product or service to sell.
d) The knowledge and experience to effectively consult with the client and internal staff.

The consultative style is most effective with high end offers.

> *Because of the ever changing value proposition and service bundle, superior selling organizations are constantly renegotiating their relationships with their customers.*

Earlier in my career, I was in senior management for a national food company. One day I fielded a phone call from one of our regional managers who had secured a high level meeting with the vice president at one of the nation's leading retailers. He asked if I would take the meeting with him in Minneapolis. Knowing we did not have much traction with the customer in the past, I agreed.

When meeting with the decision maker, I spent about 45 minutes asking some provocative questions such as, "What are some of your overarching corporate initiatives? What are you trying to accomplish in your department?" These were high level, strategic questions that had nothing to do with our category of products. As the customer answered the questions, my regional manager knew to remain completely silent.

After the client had ranted for a while, I came to understand his core problems and why our company had not taken a foothold in his stores. His organization did not have the collective bandwidth to manage the category. They simply did not have the resources.

So I asked him a simple question: "What if we put a category manager in your office to manage the category for you?" I will never forget the customer's response. He said, "You mean you would do that for me?" I said, "Sure, if we had every case, in every division, in every store, every week of the year." We left the meeting with a multi-million dollar commitment at which time I had the regional manager buy me a really big steak!

Thus a tactical relationship was built into a strategic one that would have far reaching implications for both organizations. Salespeople engaged in strategic selling techniques have to be capable of consulting *within* their own companies. They have to be advocates for their customers, ensuring their company has the required infrastructure in the form of operations, accounting, etc. to support customer initiatives. In the hypercompetitive marketplace, companies are seeking to reduce their capacity and labor. Such opportunities abound for creative vendors who take the time to understand customer's business issues.

> In B2B environments, it is incumbent on the provider to own the customer relationship, and not allow the salesperson to own it exclusively.

> The more relationships you have within an organization, the less vulnerable you are to change (such as losing your primary advocate within a client company).

As salespeople need to acquire the skills to have conversations with senior decision makers, senior executives from selling organizations need to be in the field often to ask these questions and hear the answers from the horse's mouth. Bringing a senior manager to a customer meeting is a great tactic to secure time with a decision maker.

Important information including the customer's personal habits, preferences and interests *must* be kept in a central database (typically

CRM software). Otherwise, the salesperson owns the relationship and any new salesperson working with that customer must start from scratch.

Once a more strategic relationship is built, salespeople can go deep and wide into an organization and influence many people.

The skill set of asking good questions is the preface to discovering latent needs that can be converted into service innovation and a sustainable competitive advantage.

> *Selling is about asking the right questions and converting the customer's answers into actionable outcomes that deepen the relationship.*

Business development cannot be reduced to the tactical approaches taken by the salesperson. An integrated marketing approach would include timely mailings, newsletters, blogs, viral marketing campaigns and other media intended to keep a brand relevant, delivered at times that are in sync with the selling process. Sales organizations are most successful when management has laid a foundation for personal organization, follow through, productivity and learning.

Unless there is a culture of sharing and learning among salespeople, there will always be the separation of the haves and have-nots. Such separation promotes turnover of sales people who struggle to succeed. Even in smaller companies (less than $50 million), we have clients who pay salespeople $400,000 per year or more because they eat what they kill. Sometimes these are the same salespeople who have a cavalier attitude about working within a team or sharing information.

> *Customer relationships and key information about them is the intellectual property of the company; not the salesperson.*

The modern salesperson understands that relationship building is more than golf and lunch. It is about melding personal relationships with business relationships that transcend the individuals involved and allow the opportunity for their organizations to improve to their mutual benefit.

The same is true for market intelligence. Sales organizations and senior managers should come together often to discuss what they are seeing or hearing in the marketplace as it relates to customers, competitors, etc.

A rich environment for market intelligence is trade shows and conferences. Every conference should be followed up with a debriefing where everything that is learned is shared and opportunities or threats are identified.

What do you do with market intelligence? Let it shape your thinking in the pursuit of game-changing strategies, which is the subject of the next chapter.

Chapter 10 Review

Tips for Success ...

- Make sure your marketing staff has the capabilities to manage a marketing effort based on current marketing techniques including viral and Internet marketing.

- If you sell in a B2B or high end environment, train your salespeople in consultative selling techniques. Do not allow salespeople to own the relationships. Senior executives need to listen to customers to identify opportunities for innovation.

- Successful salespeople ask the right questions and convert the answers into actionable outcomes that further the client relationship.

Chapter

11

The Building Blocks of Strategic Planning

"Plans are worthless, but planning is everything."
— Dwight D. Eisenhower

This chapter (and those that follow) will provide a framework for strategic planning and for measuring specific outcomes (execution). We are sharing some of our secret sauce in hopes that others will use these approaches in their pursuit of game changing strategies.

> *A company is like a symphony orchestra with lots of moving parts. A strategic plan can be viewed as the sheet of music that brings various functional departments together on the same page so that they can create music in harmony.*

Alchemy in strategic thinking is achieved when the CEO can focus on four or five initiatives that will drive future growth and profitability.

Strategic planning is a mechanism by which an organization gains consensus on how to apply resources, including capital and time, and to address the most important opportunities. The success or failure of a strategic plan is reliant upon stakeholders buying into the process. The earlier the organization engages them, the greater the probability to achieve the desired result.

Following are a list of building blocks commonly used in the development of a strategic plan:

PRE-MEETING PREPARATION

Objectives of Planning

The question of when and how often companies should engage in strategic planning is a subject of some interpretation. As illustrated with Amazon and others, best-in-class companies view strategic planning as a process and not an event and update their plan continuously.

At the very least, companies should reserve time for dedicated thought at least once per year or whenever there are material changes to the business, such as taking part in an acquisition. For some, the motivation for planning may be to address specific problems or opportunities; for others, it may serve a more holistic purpose.

Off-site meetings, such as those typically dedicated to strategic planning, often represent the only quality time that a team spends together out of the office. Such meetings present the opportunity for personal and professional relationships to be transformed or reinvigorated.

Some companies combine strategic planning with team building or leadership development. If there is deep dysfunction within a team, personal agendas can sabotage a strategic planning effort. It is best to try to address or mitigate these problems before a strategic planning meeting or to use the off-site as an opportunity to gain clarity and unity.

CEOs often ask me who they should invite to their strategic meetings. There are two criteria that trump all others:

- Who is capable of thinking strategically?
- Who can you trust with sensitive information?

Some use inclusion in such meetings as a reward to valued executives and staff, and exclusion as a coaching opportunity for those who don't make the grade. If there are stakeholders who are not invited to a strategic planning meeting but are important in terms of its execution, the facilitator should interview them to gain their insights and include their views in shaping the agenda.

Hiring a Facilitator

Any successful meeting has a facilitator (even if that is an internal resource). In making the decision to hire a professional, consider this analogy. Generally, a controller or CFO will maintain the books of a business. That means 90% of the work is done internally. But, when it is time to plan for taxes or file a return, most companies hire experts in the form of an accounting firm. Which is more likely to have a material effect on the value of your business: your tax liability in a given year; or, creation of the value proposition that will create strategic advantage in the marketplace?

A seasoned strategic planning facilitator will produce a more productive planning process. It is less important to find one with expertise in your industry, and more important to find one whose methodology and style will promote your objectives. Most importantly, it is vital to find someone who can work with your team and within your environment. You should also look for a facilitator who is committed to the long-term success of your plan, and will help develop a systematic approach to ensure that it is carried out.

Pre-Work

Participants, especially those who have not been through strategic planning, may experience some anxiety about the process. Old school managers who think in transactional terms don't gravitate toward such meetings and will use time as an excuse. Steps can be taken to ensure that participants are in a productive frame of mind.

Pre-work presents an opportunity for learning. In those cases in which leadership development is a specific objective, one way to break the ice is to have team members read a short leadership or strategy book (such as this one) in preparation for the retreat.

The agenda should be sent out several weeks in advance with clear direction on who should prepare which materials. A letter from the CEO explaining the overarching objectives of the meeting will provide some context. If you are ordering books or reading materials, it is best to give people 5–6 weeks to read them. If participants are to bring nothing, communicate that they are to bring nothing.

The agenda should follow a logical progression, starting with more visionary topics and exercises (like SWOT or STEEP) and conclude with specific tactics including a fully flushed out action plan. You may have team members communicate what their objectives are in advance so that various stakeholders have the opportunity to shape the content of the agenda. It is important that topics regarding infrastructure such as technology and human resources be given ample time.

The more serious you take the preparation, and the more rich the data presented, the better the assumptions made in your plan will be. For clients doing formal strategic planning for the first time, an entry point for information to collect and present would be:

* Customer feedback data
* Client segmentation analysis
* Financial statements
* Operations reports
* Profitability analysis

In smaller companies who do not practice open book management, senior managers may not be comfortable sharing financial data. An off-site retreat is the perfect time to improve the financial acumen of managers who do not understand financial reporting. If applicable, a scaled down version that demonstrates gross profit can be provided in lieu of financial statements.

Customer segmentation (the percentage of business done in each segment, preferably with margin and net profit calculations) is critical if you expect to make reasoned decisions on how to allocate resources to each segment.

Meeting Preparations

It is always preferable to conduct such a meeting off-site, as participants will struggle to shut out office distractions and focus on the task at hand. The further in advance you book a venue, the more likely you are to get the desired space. If you choose to have the meeting in your office, communicate that anyone disrupting the meeting will be wished the best of luck in their next position, wherever that might be.

Choose a meeting space (with natural light) that is the appropriate size for the number of participants. Make sure that it has a decent sized conference table and ample space on the wall to hang tear sheets if you choose to use them. I may be old school in this regard, but participants often find it useful to reference notes throughout the meeting. Tear pad sheets (Post-it style) create a more creative environment than merely keeping notes on a computer.

Like a good airline pilot, make a checklist of the materials you need to bring including easels, flip charts, markers, computer equipment and a projector. If you are going to be meeting in a hotel, thoughtful preparation can easily save hundreds of dollars in meeting and materials costs.

MEETING COMPONENTS

❖ ❖ ❖

Mission and Values

All elements of an organization's strategic plan are a reflection of its mission and values. Simply put, the mission clarifies the organization's purpose, and values are how you wish to behave. Some organizations also construct a "Vision Statement" which is an articulation of what the organization would like to become when the strategic plan materializes.

Mission Statements articulate what products and services the company wishes to offer and to whom. To arrive at a mission statement, have participants list three or four word phrases that describe your commitments (i.e. commitment to quality, service, customer satisfaction, etc.). A mission statement should answer the question, "What are we here to do?" Try to avoid canned and overused phrases such as "premier" and "leading." A mission statement does not have to be lengthy. Here are some clear and concise mission statements:

Apple: "Apple is committed to bringing the best personal computing experience to students, educators, creative professionals and consumers around the world through its innovative hardware, software and Internet offerings."

Nike: "To bring inspiration and innovation to every athlete in the world."

John F. Kennedy: "This nation should dedicate itself to achieving the goal, before this decade is out, of landing a man on the moon and returning him safely to Earth."

If the group has difficulty finding the exact verbiage, table the conversation for a small working group (three or four people at the most) to finalize language.

Accomplishments

A good way to begin a strategy meeting is by having attendees list their company or team accomplishments. This puts the participants in a positive frame of mind and engages them in discussion early in the meeting.

STEEP Exercise & Scenario Planning

We described the thinking behind STEEP exercises in Chapter 4. A STEEP exercise is a method used to consider environmental factors external to the organization. To complete a STEEP Analysis, have the participants list the Social, Technological, Ecological, Economic and Political trends that may affect your business in the next 3–5 years.

After completing the STEEP Exercise, have the participants complete a forced ranking of which of the trends are most likely to occur and combine them into the most likely scenarios. Assuming you have time, consider other specific scenarios (positive and negative) and what your team would do should they come to fruition. This exercise often helps to promote strategic thinking and various initiatives that may be undertaken in preparation for changes in the operating environment.

Scenario planning is very difficult without a seasoned facilitator. Whatever method you chose, challenge your participants to think through the ramifications of these scenarios.

Customer Advisory Panels

A review of sales productivity and the organization's relationship with its customers or stakeholders can take on several forms. One extremely effective method (when practical) is convening a Customer Advisory Panel.

Generally four to five customers are positioned at the front of the room and asked a series of scripted questions that they received in advance. The questions should be forward facing, focused on what improvements could be made in the future to improve the company's value proposition.

The other participants should be coached not to speak at all during this discussion. They should have time to ask questions of the panel after the scripted questions are asked and answered. A Customer Advisory Panel is an excellent starting point for a retreat as it sets the tone for the meeting (as customer centric). From a practical standpoint, it provides information that can be used in your planning and is conducted before confidential information about your company is posted throughout the room.

Market Segmentation and Sales Review

Well managed sales organizations are adept at segmenting customers and measuring sales growth, profit, and profit growth by sector, as well as projecting which markets they wish to address. We have had many instances with clients when such an analysis revealed sectors and customers that were not profitable at all.

Sales productivity reports are also valuable, especially if the meeting participants are not often privy to such information. Metrics that reveal selling effectiveness such as number of sales calls, close ratios and new customer growth can be reported and analyzed as predictive indicators.

Operations Review

While often sales is the sizzle; it is operations that is the steak. A review of operational results generally includes evaluation of metrics such as average cycle time, fill rate, and defects.

There is often a triangulating effect between departments such as operations, sales, engineering, design, etc. Companies manage these triangles with varying degrees of effectiveness. A strategic meeting is an appropriate time to discuss the role of each functional department and how various teams can best work with each other to improve processes.

In manufacturing, it is those companies that have leaned out their operations that have survived the onslaught of price competition. You can only cut into your operations so deep before cutting into muscle and bone. While Six Sigma and lean manufacturing are immensely powerful, they are not all encompassing (they focus more to the efficiency of operations, than to top line growth).

It is important that the operations team understands the decisions made regarding the tradeoffs made in the value proposition. For example, if a company chooses to be customer intimate, it may have to handle more than the optimal level of inventory to fill orders. The appropriate level of investment may not be an operations decision; it may be a leadership team decision.

Conversely, such meetings can lay the groundwork for functional departments such as sales and accounting to gain an understanding of how they can contribute to greater efficiency in operations leading to improved customer experiences.

SWOT

The analysis of Strengths, Weaknesses, Opportunities and Threats is the most common strategic planning exercise. Strengths and weaknesses represent internal factors; and opportunities and threats measure external factors. Within our firm, we generally conduct a variant we refer to as "Competitive SWOT."

To complete a Competitive SWOT, consider not only strengths, weaknesses, opportunities and threats for your company but those of your top competitors. By putting yourself in their shoes, you gain a new perspective on how they may approach you as a competitor and how they may enhance their goods and services. If your market is highly fractured, it may be more productive to combine similar competitors and consider competing models as opposed to specific companies. For example, you might consider "large chain restaurants" as opposed to Ruby Tuesday.

Note that as the STEEP Exercise and SWOT both examine external factors, to complete them both can be redundant. One approach is to combine STEEP with internal issues and opportunities to achieve a similar output.

Organizational Survey

In advance of a retreat, it is useful to query the participants on issues affecting the organization. Depending upon the nature of the organization, questions may range on topics from marketing to operations and learning and growth.

An organizational survey is an unobtrusive way to identify problems and opportunities. Occasionally, participants will share things in an anonymous survey that they will not share in a strategic meeting. Among the most difficult challenges facing the professional facilitator is overcoming the denial and biases of senior managers. Sometimes the organizational survey provides insights on the elephants in the room. It is also more productive to work through a documented list of organizational issues rather than to just list them at random in a meeting format.

Overarching Organizational Initiatives

Perhaps the most critical outcome of a strategic planning retreat is for the participants to agree on the initiatives that the organization will pursue. These mandates are initiatives that typically require a commitment of resources and collaboration across functional departments over an extended period of time. Organizations can only effectively manage a handful of initiatives at one time.

One method for gaining consensus on which initiatives to choose is known as a "forced prioritization." By creating a list of initiatives on a tear pad, the group can weigh the importance of each initiative by taking a vote using dots or a marker. It is generally clear which are the most important to the group and which are of lesser priority.

Strategies and Tactics

Strategies and tactics were concepts first used by military leaders in the Roman Empire (strategy translates to army in Greek).[43] Strategies were initially defined as the decisions on which battles should be fought and tactics were how they would be fought. In a simplified management application, strategies could be thought of as what businesses you wish to be in, and what tools you need to possess to execute your strategy. Tactics relate the specific actions you will take to bring your strategies to life.

Marketing Plan

In Chapter 8, we illustrated the changing face of marketing and how organizations must adapt. The concepts of marketing and strategic planning are somewhat "chicken and egg" as marketers will have you believe that the marketing department should drive strategy based on their unique understanding of the marketplace. There may be some truth to that, but strategic decisions must be made within the context of the organization's capabilities, resources and factors that may be outside marketing's purview. A distinction must be made between strategic planning and marketing strategy.

At a strategic planning meeting, the senior marketing executive should have an outline of marketing initiatives that they expect or propose to launch. He or she should also be open to the likelihood that the company's marketing investment and priorities could change based on the vision created in the strategic plan.

Five-Year Growth Plans

For-profits are typically either focused on growing the top line, improving the bottom line, or both. When prompted to name the source of future growth, clients often cannot clearly articulate volume growth targets by market segment. Once a business reaches a mature place on the S Curve, growth becomes more difficult to sustain. A key deliverable of strategic planning should be to set growth targets and to ascertain from where the growth will come.

The entrepreneurial instinct is to offer new products or services for sale. When new products are presented as a line extension, the cost to market is lower than creating a new brand. An overwhelming number of brand extensions fail; not only in terms of new product sales, but also in terms of diluting existing products.

In consumer products, only 1% of products reach $100 million in revenue in the first year (which might sound like a lot, but given the budgets of companies such as Campbell's and General Mills, this is a paltry sum).[44] The R&D investment required to support product development is limiting to smaller firms.

For new products to be accepted in the marketplace, they must have a strong brand identity, differentiated through distinctive claims (more nutritious, etc.). Thus new products need to be thought out carefully. Even then, sales projections should be very conservative.

As a means for growth, mergers and acquisitions have even a smaller payoff.[45] One study demonstrated that after an acquisition, on average:

- Sales growth dropped 6.0%
- EBIT growth fell 9.4%
- Market Cap growth decreased 2.5%

There seems to be an exception during downturns, when mergers yield (on average) 15% higher returns.[46] While the motivation for most mergers is cost savings and efficiencies, the best time to complete an acquisition is when there is a synergistic relationship between the two businesses that will drive top line revenue.

Among the strategies that can be employed to build sales within an organization, organic growth is typically the least expensive to create.

Strategy Maps

Executives often complain to us that their underlings are incapable of executing strategy. They are often the same ones that acknowledge that they have not invested adequate time in explaining the future direction of the company.

We often use visual aids to communicate strategies. In Chapter 3, there is an example of a Futures Map (or strategy map) that simply illustrates the ideal future the company is trying to create. A strategy map can be used to explain the strategy to a partner, employee, vendor or customer.

The Action Plan

In the absence of clear directives, everything is a priority. Often, mid-managers and front line employees are unclear about the organization's top priorities.

Before leaving any meeting (strategic or otherwise), there should be complete agreement on who will do what and when. The best action plans are developed and organized by initiative. If sorted by action item, it is easy to lose sight of the overarching initiatives you are trying to achieve.

An action plan can typically have two or three tiers. You can organize by initiative and action, or by strategy, tactic and action.

	Strategy & Tactics	Champion	Due Date	Assisted By
	Lead our industry in customer loyalty			
2	Goal: Achieve 75% retention by 2010			
	Tactic: Integrate CRM			
2A	Hire CRM Consultant	Tom	5/1/2010	Jim
2B	Complete integration of SalesForce	Tom	12/1/2010	Jim
	Tactic: Survey Clients on Satisfaction			
2C	Establish survey process	Phil	2/1/2010	Carol
2D	Acquire survey tool	Karen	4/1/2010	John
2E	Complete test of 50 clients	Karen	6/1/2010	John

KPIs/Scorecards

The majority of key performance indicators should be specifically linked to the organization's strategic initiatives. KPIs (as well as things like departmental goals and the performance management system) are outputs of the strategy. They are the numbers that measure the company's ability to execute. Companies with strong business intelligence absorb less risk, as the path to profitability is clearer.

Organizations are often overly reliant on commonly accepted financial metrics (a form of collective myopia). What is the metric that most people use to measure their fitness and attractiveness? They use weight, which is a flawed measurement because muscle weighs more than fat. Body fat is a much more accurate depiction of fitness, but weight is much easier to measure, so we all choose the path of least resistance (even though most gyms have a system for measuring body fat).

Best-in-class companies make the investments in infrastructure to extract relevant and timely KPIs. A company of any scale (say $25 million in revenue) certainly warrants having finance personnel dedicated to developing business intelligence such as KPIs. An investment in an entry level analyst will yield a return on investment through improved margins or reduced costs (assuming you have access to valid information). In preparing for a strategy meeting, it is a worthwhile investment to take the steps necessary to extract key indicators from which you can make important management decisions.

Establishing Core Competencies

Core competencies transcend the skill sets that often describe an individual's abilities. They speak to the infrastructure built to support service of a business discipline. As in the case of Walmart, the competency is supply chain efficiency; in the case of Southwest, asset utilization (the planes are generally full and on time).

Best-in-class organizations build the ability to hire, retain and develop based on the competencies that serve customers best. These skills are honed over time, and built into tribal knowledge.

The need for core competencies should drill down deep into tactics including the design of performance reviews, training and office design. The strategic plan should identify key competencies that require development and expansion.

Performance Management Should Integrate with the Strategy

As we will document later, the most profitable companies create a relationship between the business strategy, and how employees are evaluated and compensated (see Chapter 12). The execution of strategy and optimizing employee performance are inter-dependent.

For a company to be a product or service innovator, candidate selection, training and performance appraisal systems should be in alignment and promote that competency. When setting departmental or individual goals, employees should be identifying goals that directly correlate with corporate objectives.

Strategic Planning Documentation

Output from a strategic planning meeting should be circulated to the participants within several days of the off-site. People need to see the strategy converted into operational terms, as validation that they have received a return on their investment (time and energy). The faster people have access to the documents, the faster they will begin implementation. Include an Executive Summary, Strategy Map and Action Plan toward the front of the document so that readers can conduct a quick scan of the strategy.

Contingency Planning

I once heard Jim Tunney a Super Bowl referee give a speech in which he said, "refereeing in the NFL is striving for perfection, knowing that you will never achieve it." Even the most thorough strategists cannot plan for every possible eventuality. Organizations must be agile enough to react to the unplanned.

At 7:00 p.m. on every weekday, a group of managers gather at UPS's Worldport facility in Louisville, Kentucky. During a conference call, the group deploys "hot crews" of stand by workers and up to 20 aircraft at the ready in the event of service interruption on the part of one of its "Browntail" aircraft.[47] The importance of such customer care was the driver to UPS founder Jim Casey coining the phrase "Constructive Dissatisfaction" to represent his compulsion with satisfying customers, even at the expense of profit.

Smaller companies may not have the wherewithal to have stand-by crews at the ready, but should consider how they may apply certain resources in the event of short term events or calamities such as electrical outage, or shortage of raw materials.

Post Planning Follow-Up

The process of strategic planning itself creates few outcomes other than agreement on various decisions. The real lift from strategic thinking comes as a result of the actions that follow.

A best practice for reinforcing strategic thinking is to meet monthly or weekly to review the action plan and KPIs. This is particularly important right after a strategic retreat, when the focus on deliverables is fresh. Follow-up meetings are a way to create some rhythm around the strategic plan and to engrain strategic thinking into the culture (a method practiced relentlessly at Amazon, for instance) which promotes achievement of specific and intentional outcomes.

In a high trust culture, failure to meet a deliverable is not met with anger or disappointment but with focus on what has to happen to solve the problems and move forward the initiatives. There is no shame in moving deadlines (unless there are material, financial or customer implications), but there is shame in not communicating why they are not met. In a performance culture, people are responsible for getting things done and are not afraid to ask for help in achieving organizational objectives.

Communication with people who were not included in the off-site is critical. The people back in the office who have not been privy to the particulars of the meeting can be thinking almost anything. Some will think your meeting is merely a boondoggle or that you are conspiring to eliminate jobs, etc.

To create alignment around the plan requires that you clearly articulate the strategy to stakeholders. Employees need to understand how their role relates to the grander scheme. The sooner that senior management can debrief employees, the better.

Early Wins

Many action plans tend to be front loaded, as participants feel confident about their ability to complete a multitude of tasks immediately following the planning meeting. One way to create buzz and reinforce the value of planning is to gain early wins. Focus on completing one or two initiatives right away so that your senior team feels a sense of accomplishment.

Walking the Walk

For reasons that will become obvious, the identities of the company and individuals I am about to describe will remain nameless.

Early in my career, I had an experience that shaped my thinking on mission and values. Out of business school, I went into the food business. At the raw age of 30, I was running a division of food stores in California. It was an extraordinary responsibility to manage 27 P&Ls for a public company. But I was not privy to nor did I have the depth of understanding at that age to comprehend the magnitude of my company's financial problems. About a year later, our stores were up for sale.

One day, I fielded a call from a gentleman, who I will call Jim, who said that he intended to acquire my business unit, and that he was extremely impressed with our business operations. He wanted to talk to me about coming to work for him. At about that time, my employer filed bankruptcy and Jim and I were subpoenaed to testify in bankruptcy court in Texas. We decided to fly together to discuss the transition. Over a hot dog in the airport snack bar, Jim offered me a position in his organization.

The purpose of the proceeding was to approve the transaction (which included significant California real estate), and the creditors were seeking to protect their interests. When Jim took the stand, the creditors' attorney asked him point blank, "Do you intend to operate these stores or sell them off piece meal," implying that if treated as individual assets, they may have a greater value. Jim, responded, "We will operate these stores as long as they are profitable to us" (these are not his exact words, I am paraphrasing).

On our flight back to California, we had a toast and finalized a plan to move over to the newly combined company. Jim would stop in my office occasionally. I was like his new puppy dog. He was a kind man and I liked him personally. Meanwhile, the stores that my new company had acquired were being sold off piece meal, which really made me question the intentions of my new employer. Another year passed before things crystallized for me.

We had run an ad for a big brand cereal that was supported with an online coupon (meaning there were no physical coupons, every time a box was scanned, the consumer received a discount). I reported in a weekly marketing meeting that the promotion had underperformed against our expectations and we had an excess of inventory left on hand. The President of the company approached me after the meeting and told me that it would be a lot better if we overstated our sales in our reporting to the manufacturer, thereby increasing the amount of our rebate.

That afternoon I went to our CFO. I told him that I considered the request improper and I would not overstate our sales in our reporting to the manufacturer. The President backed down, but I knew I was not long for this world and quickly left to go to work for a vendor.

Thus I learned at a young age that integrity is not something that is written in a values statement; it is something you practice every day, because your employees and customers expect it, and your business depends on it.

I recently had a client who was trying to craft a values statement, and integrity was offered as one of the potential values. One of the executives in the room made a stunning observation, "If we are going to list integrity as a core value, we need to stop lying to our customers." I was shocked at the comment, especially because I knew that my client did not intend to be disingenuous.

If you are going to take the time to do strategic planning, and to develop mission and values statements, you need to walk the walk. If you expect others to take values or other facets of your planning seriously, you have to lead by example.

Integrity is something I think about regularly in my practice. I have one guiding principle that has served me well over the years.

We do the right thing for the client, even when the recommendations we make are not the most lucrative for our firm.

Special Note for the Non-Profit Sector

As of this writing, I serve on three non-profit boards. Such organizations have a special place in my heart. The strategic plan for a non-profit is materially similar to that of a for-profit. The primary differences are:

- The non-profit is beholden to a different set of stakeholders including the community it services, government agencies, and its donors.
- The services provided by the non-profit need to be evaluated not within a context of profit but within whatever criteria are consistent with its charter.
- Often, some of the heavy lifting is done by volunteers who are not accountable to specific outcomes. Generally, the non-profit has very few resources.
- The consumer of the strategic plan is often external stakeholders.

A similar format as described above works equally well within the non-profit sector.

Chapter 11 Review

- Every strategic planning meeting should be managed by a facilitator.

- Conduct outreach with stakeholders in advance to gather information and include them in the process.

- Use pre-work as an opportunity for learning.

- Publish the meeting agenda well in advance.

- Every meeting should yield a clear set of deliverables.

- Organize the output into 6–8 initiatives and an action plan complete with deliverables, champions and dates.

- Schedule follow-up meetings to communicate the plan to others and follow up on the action plan and KPIs.

12

The Magic Bullet: Creating Alignment through Scorecarding

"Management is doing things right; leadership is doing the right things."

— PETER DRUCKER

Several years ago I had surgery on my shoulder, due in part to my stubborn refusal to acknowledge that basketball is not a game meant for middle-aged men. Unable to do many things I love, including weight lifting, tennis and basketball, I took up cycling. I went and bought a ridiculously expensive performance road bike with all the gear. After putting on the tight fitting clothing for the first time, I walked down the stairs to have my 14-year-old daughter look up and me and say, "Dad, you go take that off right now!"

My daughter lacked context on why I would possibly wear such hideous clothing, clearly a decision that would impact her greatly, as I would be an embarrassment to her and all her friends. She lacked the texture and understanding of why cycling was important to me and ultimately to her, as I hope to be healthy in the later years of my life.

We simply were not aligned on what was critically important. As illustrated with the contrast of Coca-Cola and McDonald's, a lack of alignment can be an extremely expensive proposition.

> *Without alignment, you cannot have true accountability because there is no agreement from people to what they should be held accountable.*

It is hard to objectively define what makes a culture of alignment, but we all know it when we see it. Every person reading these words has either worked within an organization where people seemed to have a common set of goals, or in one where everyone was out for themselves. With alignment comes a special energy, where employees are motivated and driven to meet company, departmental and individual goals, and share commitment in satisfying customers.

Among the most dynamic changes that have occurred in the last decade are that behemoth companies such as General Electric, Microsoft and Walmart are holding vendors accountable to specific measurable performance outcomes. If you are a vendor shipping Walmart laundry detergent, your company is required to satisfy a broad spectrum of vendor requirements, including on-time delivery and fill rate.

To remain a vendor in good standing with Walmart, suppliers must meet very high standards (98–99% service level on many products). Once new standards are reached, the bar is lifted again. In Walmart's case, customer satisfaction is a moving target.

If you are a vendor to one of these companies, the only way to survive is to hold your vendors and employees accountable to rigorous performance standards. To meet a 98% service level with such a customer, you must demand a 99% service level from suppliers in the hopes that you will only lose 1% in productivity along the way.

More rigorous accountability is cascading through our economy. Customer expectations are heightened every day as customers adjust to the service level afforded them by companies such as Nordstrom, Lexus and UPS. Professional buyers' personal experiences translate to their expectations in B2B commerce.

Like capitalism itself, the prototypical corporation is the best system we have, yet it is often terribly flawed. Silos are a natural by-product of functional departments such as accounting, engineering, sales and operations.

As Patrick Lencioni points out in the "Five Dysfunction's" model (see *The Five Dysfunctions of a Team*), business results can be significantly restricted by dysfunctional relationships within a team, or across functional departments. Without trust, you cannot have commitment and buy-in. Without buy-in you cannot achieve a focus on results.

Team dysfunction encumbers the execution of strategy. Within the methodology we advocate, teams must work together to create the metrics to which they will be held accountable.

> *If there is a magic bullet in the execution of*
> *strategy, it is the concept of scorecarding.*

There are significant differences between the treatment of key performance indicators (KPIs) used in most organizations and the use of metrics in a scorecarding system. KPIs are generally viewed by a handful of people in a small or medium sized business. The concept of scorecarding provides for a methodology where the entire company is managed through a set of published numbers. Most importantly, these numbers are a derivative of the strategy, and track results that will drive company initiatives.

Most KPIs that I see in small and medium sized firms (and especially in those companies that are not operationally excellent) are financial metrics. Imagine you were playing a baseball game. When your financials come out, say on the tenth of the month, what inning of the game would it be? The game would be over. There would be no opportunity to affect the outcome. You could not decide who pitches, who hits or if you want to hit and run. By the time financials come out and adjustments are made to various processes, a month or two have passed before problems can be solved.

> *Financial metrics are critical, but have an inherent*
> *limitation; they are historical in nature.*

Walk into any manufacturing plant and there is always one number hanging on the wall. It is generally some variant of days since lost time injury, or number of injuries, etc. The employer provides this number as a message to their employees: if this number ever changes from a 0 to 1, you are all going to spend the rest of your life in OSHA training! The employer generally provides training and develops procedures that reinforce specific behaviors (in this case safety) that they wish to promote.

A scorecard can affect behavior for a broader range of constituents. The framework captures the expectations of internal and external customers and measures the organization's ability to meet them. The scorecard converts the vision of the organization into operational terms, and measures the drivers of business value.

It is important to make a distinction between these concepts and *The Balanced Scorecard*, the ingenious work of Robert Kaplan and David Norton of Harvard Business School. It is estimated that as many as half of Fortune 500 companies have used some form of *The Balanced Scorecard* including industry leaders such as GE, Microsoft, Exxon Mobil and Time Warner.

Kaplan and Norton built the methodology to address a pervasive problem in business today: less than 10% of formulated strategies are actually executed.[48] Kaplan and Norton, in their numerous books, have reported extraordinary results in their use of *The Balanced Scorecard.*

The word "balanced" refers to Kaplan and Norton's assertion that metrics should typically be measured across four dimensions: financial, customer, process and learning and growth, and balance both lagging and leading indicators. Seventy-five percent of the average company's value comes from intangible assets, things that cannot be measured in a financial statement.[49]

Within our firm, we use concepts similar to *The Balanced Scorecard*, in combination with other best practices and have formed a methodology simply referred to here as scorecarding. One of the reasons our firm has been so successful is that there are relatively few practitioners that focus on implementing this methodology in smaller and medium sized firms (it is our differentiator).

Many companies try to do it themselves and fail because they are focused on the wrong things and try to implement Kaplan and Norton's methodology without deviation. Senior managers (who are accustomed to silos) can become very passionate about which numbers are right and which are wrong. Their zeal to come up with the perfect numbers defeats the process. They become frustrated with the intricacies and they just quit.

Leading Indicators	Lagging Indicators
Customer Satisfaction	Revenue per Employee
Employee Satisfaction	Employee Turnover
Website Traffic	Conversion Rate (Web Visitors)
RFQs Submitted	RFQs Accepted
New Account Applications	New Accounts
Sales Calls	Revenue Growth %
Customer Touches (A Customers)	New Customers +$100K Sales
New Opportunities (in CRM)	New Customers-Segment ABC
New Account Applications	Account Receivables (Average Days)
Marketing Events	Conversion Rate-Sales Calls
Capacity (Hours, Percent, etc.)	Margin %-Segment XYZ
Cycle Time-Days to Deliver	Number of Active Customers
Machine Up-Time	Cost Per Unit Shipped
Preventive Maintenance	Defects
Inventory Aging	Raw Materials Inventory
Training Hours per Employee	Line of Credit Drawn
Labor Hours	Labor % of Units Produced
Overtime Hours	Labor % of Sales

Our guidance to clients is that perfection is overrated. In building out a scorecard, there is nothing to gain by being so consumed with selecting the right numbers that you lose sight of the broader opportunity. The numbers are far less important than the way the numbers are used. In a simplified form, such a methodology does not require fancy graphs or complex computer systems. The most important factor in the development of metrics is that they be constructed by the team that will be measured by them.

The magic in scorecarding is the ability to view the results of corporate initiatives in real time. It is common for organizations to pursue multiple directives concurrently, such as revenue growth, margin optimization or cost cutting strategies.

One of the more remarkable outcomes of scorecarding is the ability to determine cause and affect relationships. Your scorecard can be used to diagnose problems quickly and push decision making throughout the organization. Good scorecard measurements track critical success factors.

Thus, there is a distinction between a purely financial metric such as "costs" and a scorecarding measurement which is a predictive indicator of cost, illustrated as:

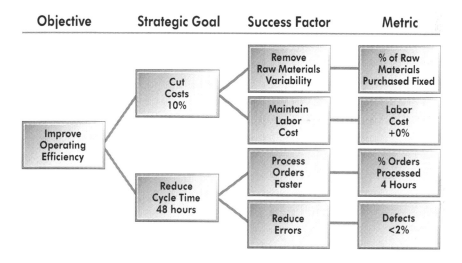

We advocate that KPIs or scorecards should:

a) Include predictive indicators including those numbers that are customer centric and predict profitability.

b) Be public and predominantly displayed.

c) Be measured in real time (generally monthly or weekly).

d) Be explained in depth to employees so that they can make better business decisions.

e) Be the basis for company celebrations.

f) Be the basis for incentives and bonuses.

Following is an example of a simple scorecard for the fictional Z Vitamin Company:

Measure	Q1 Target	JAN	FEB	MAR	% Attained
Financial					
$ Receivables +60 Days in arrears	$85,000	$103,000	$90,123	$84,000	33%
Margin Custom Shipments	55.0%	52.5%	53.5%	55.1%	33%
Sales per CS representative	$50,000	$44,154	$47,234	$47,388	0%
Customer					
Monthly shipments custom	$300,000	$284,000	$304,000	$312,000	67%
Average customer shipments	$75.00	$71.00	$72.00	$73.05	0%
Call Center inbound calls	25,000	23,5000	23,750	27,400	33%
CS up sell rates	50%	55%	52%	52%	100%
New customers acquired	300	312	333	340	100%
Net Promoter Score	40%	33%	38%	40%	33%
Internal Process					
Custom cycle time	3	3.7	29	2.9	37%
Volume manufacturing cycle time	2	1.9	1.9	1.8	100%
Equipment uptime (lost hours)	24	23	16	9	100%
Shipping error percent	1.0%	2.0%	0.5%	0.4%	67%
Learning and Growth					
% performance reviews on time	100%	75%	100%	100%	67%
Lost time injuries	0	0	0	1	67%
Training hours per FTE upselling	4	0	4	4	67%
Average Score					**58%**

Companies vary in their use of dimensions (such as customer or internal process in *The Balanced Scorecard* model), targets, formats and frequency. Often the structure is a function of resources and the organization's ability to export information from various systems.

In professional football, there is a predictive indicator (also referred to as leading indicator) that football coaches use to predict the winners of football games. They know that the team with the least turnovers wins a National Football League game 78% of the time, more than the teams with the most rushing yards (73%), time of possession (70%) or total yards (68%). The desired outcome (points scored) is directly correlated with the number of turnovers.[50]

Thus NFL coaches go to great lengths to draft quarterbacks who have low interception ratios and running backs who don't fumble. They drill constantly on how to hold on to the ball and strip it from the other team. Much of the makeup of an NFL team is built around managing turnovers. In sports, performance metrics are constantly reported in public view. In baseball, it is standard to view a hitter's batting average, home runs and RBIs when they come to the plate.

Yet in business, some executives are petrified to share any numbers at all with employees, and loath benchmarking employees against each other only, enabling a silo mentality.

Corporations are sensitive about their operating numbers because of concern that competitors will gain access to them. The irony of this paradigm is that those companies who out execute their competitors are the ones that best leverage both the numbers and the people consuming them. If you want people to perform at a high level, they have to understand the numbers they are being held accountable to, and how they contribute to the bottom line.

Imagine you were in a business where cash flow is king. As CEO, you went to the VP of Sales and said, "Our cash flow is tight and I need you to go to your salespeople and have them make some calls to customers to see if we can collect some of these aged receivables." What do you think the typical salesperson would say? He would tell you to take a long walk off a short pier because, "I don't do collections. That is accounting's job."

> *Such a response is the very definition of a silo. Accounting does accounting, sales does sales. Imagine a different way of thinking: where sales and accounting are both responsible for sales and for accounting, and both are measured on the common threads that are strategically important.*

In such an environment, a scorecard item might be "Receivables over 60 days in arrears." Imagine that both the accounting clerk and the salesperson are partially compensated based on the company's ability to collect receivables. Wouldn't the salesperson be more likely to be an enabler to the accounting department? Might he even pick up the phone without making a fuss?

The accounting department supports sales in numerous activities from how the invoice is delivered to terms and processing expense checks. They are often responsible for reporting, or designing elements of an enterprise system that enables sales reporting. Would these functional areas be more collaborative if they shared common goals?

One of our clients is a large regional printer in Southern California, printing upscale car brochures and menus for restaurants including the Cheesecake Factory. We began scorecarding with this client in 2004. It was not long before the numbers began to sing to us like music. The client came to realize very quickly that their plate spoilage was costing several thousand dollars per month and, more importantly, was impacting their ability to deliver services within the timeline expected by their customers. After doing a deeper dive into the root cause of the problem, it was evident that there was a correlation between the reprints of plates and instances when the production staff failed to meet and preplan their jobs.

So they began to scorecard the percent of jobs over $10,000 for which a pre-planning meeting occurred. Immediately after scoring the pre-planning meetings, the number of customer errors were dramatically reduced improving the customer experience and saving tens of thousands of dollars per year. As holding the planning meetings became ingrained in the culture, the plate metric was removed and replaced with something else. In the four years that followed, the client improved profitability despite the depressed printing market.

The number one objection to scorecarding is the investment in time. What is counterintuitive is that keeping score requires less bandwidth than not keeping score. By managing against a set of predictive indicators, senior managers are not required to make all the decisions. Scorecards promote decentralized decision making. Mid-level managers know that any decision that positively affects the scorecard is the correct decision, because strategic priorities are predefined.

Sometimes CFOs embrace scorecards (as they see them as drivers of profitability) and champion the effort of scoring. Conversely, some feel overburdened by their responsibilities and do not embrace the idea of having more work to do.

> *If you had a $30 million business and believed that you could get a 2% improvement in productivity through diligent measurement, it would be a slam dunk decision to hire an analyst to manage a scorecard and provide vital business intelligence to the leadership team and others throughout the organization.*

One of the more colorful characters I have come across is Forrest Blake. Formally a very successful commercial real estate broker, Forrest had become addicted to golf, as so many of us have. He originally bought into three GolfTec franchises in Southern California.

GolfTec has a remarkable golf instruction technology whereby the student is videotaped, and every angle and position of the student's swing is analyzed side by side with Tiger Woods, or any other professional golfer. There is a virtual driving range and other cool technologies that make for a unique golf instruction experience. Yet, the Southern California stores were struggling.

Forrest, who is very entrepreneurial, saw an opportunity, and forged a new partnership with the region's franchisees. He took over a block of underperforming stores as the CEO of a newly formed

LLC. Forrest was referred to me by one of the minority owners of the newly formed entity.

Forrest felt he had to make an immediate impact to make the stores profitable, and service his debt. Most of the people coming to work for Forrest did not know him. Golf pros are not the most motivated of sorts, and this group of golf pros had never been in an environment where they were held accountable to any kind of performance measurements or specific business outcomes. This group of stores was performing well below national benchmarks, even though they were located in an affluent California region with many golfers.

Forrest didn't waste any time. He began holding a series of meetings and asked me to work with his management team to establish a "culture of accountability." GolfTec is a data driven business and has a massive amount of information available to its franchisees. The previous owners had not done much to leverage these numbers to drive performance. They were data rich, but information poor.

Forrest did something truly innovative; he took the concept of scorecarding and created a dashboard in the form of a golf scorecard with 18 metrics (a metaphor for the number of holes on a golf course).

Forrest was about to learn something that is intuitive to many, but mastered by few: the fastest way to gain alignment for an initiative is to train and measure, and manage against the measurements.

The types of things that were measured included the number of days before a follow-up phone call was made after an introductory swing analysis was provided. Forrest held weekly management meetings in which performance was measured in terms of birdies and bogies (for you non golfers, that is golf lingo for scoring above average or below average).

He had taken a management concept and converted it into language his pros could understand. Golf pros who achieved the best scores received both financial consideration, a heavy dose of praise and spiffs such as flat screen televisions. Forrest changed the culture of the organization, literally overnight.

In an exit interview of a poor performing pro, the pro said to Forrest, "I was a good performer before these scorecards came along," which is code for saying that I was just fine here before I was held accountable for specific performance outcomes.

Scorecards can be applied to almost any attribute of a business from customer satisfaction to sales and operations.

When applied correctly, a scorecard becomes the bellwether of the health of the business, predicting future growth and profitability.

Scorecards may also provide dimensions of reporting not readily available in the typical P&L.

Whenever possible, businesses should be organized as individual business units. Companies such as GE and Johnson & Johnson break down businesses by profit center so that operating efficiencies can be more readily measured (smaller business entities are easier to measure).

Some managers think that a scorecard feels like a weapon, but it can be used as a carrot instead of a stick. Accomplishments on scorecard results can be the rallying cry, and the basis for company celebrations and awards. Such celebrations not only create buy-in for the process but build camaraderie around the things deemed as strategically important, getting the entire organization swimming in the same direction. Yet perhaps the most powerful use of scorecards is as the foundation for measuring individual performance, which we will discuss in Chapter 14.

Building a scorecard for the first time can feel like a daunting task, and often companies utilize an expert. If you choose to build a scorecard yourself, start off with four or five measurements that are strategically important, predictive and you are willing to share with your employees. As we have illustrated above, a dedication to the methodology is more important than the particular numbers you select.

Chapter 12 Review

- Scorecards are a methodology for gathering real time business intelligence.

- Scorecards are different than typical financial measurements as they are based in part on predictive indicators.

- Scorecards are most useful when they are published in public view.

- Create alignment by explaining the numbers to front line staff and celebrating accomplishments.

13

Be a Best-In-Class Employer

*"In a few hundred years, when the history of
our time is written from a long term perspective,
it is likely that the most important event those
historians will see is not technology, not the
Internet, not e-commerce. It is the unprecedented
change in the human condition. For the first
time — literally — substantial and rapidly
growing numbers of people have choices. For the
first time, they will have to manage themselves.
And society is totally unprepared for it."*

— PETER DRUCKER

In this chapter we will illustrate how seemingly unrelated factors are emerging into a potential tipping point that has deep implications for the execution of strategy. The following numbers should take your breath away. Seventy-five million Americans will be eligible to retire by the year 2011.

While unemployment can occasionally spike (and is unusually high as of this writing), it is a poor measure of the health of the US workforce. It is more of an economic metric, measuring the ability of the economy to generate enough jobs to employ the least employable (that is not a criticism of the unemployed; there are many fine people looking for work in a competitive environment).

Even when unemployment is high our economy does not generate an ample number of A candidates. There is a dearth of high skilled workers, ranging from accounting to nursing and welding. In 2009, The Fortune 500 (representing 14% of the total workforce) alone had over 100,000 open positions. Our economy is in desperate need of a massive training effort to redirect displaced workers (such as in the auto industry) into new jobs where they can earn a livable wage.

We are in a form of collective myopia. We appear to be on the verge of an employment 9/11, and American businesses are completely unprepared for it.

Consider the emerging employment trends:

- With the advent of the Internet and emerging technologies, technical workers are in particular demand. While the US economy has grown 64% over the last 17 years, H-1B temporary visas for foreign workers have remained constant even though 73% of PhDs in electrical engineering and 61% in computer science are going to foreign nationals. In terms of specialized labor, the US economy is not generating enough qualified applicants.

- With the erosion of pension plans and 401Ks, coupled with longer life expectancy, Baby Boomers are facing the prospect of working deeper into retirement age. The number of employees under 55 years of age in the workforce is projected to decline through 2016 while those 65 and older will grow at an 80% clip.

- Older workers, who have been working toward retirement, will want to work in untraditional roles as consultants and in part-time jobs.

Projected Percentage Change in Labor Force by Age, 2006–2016

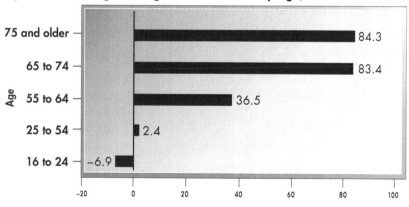

Source: U.S. Bureau of Labor Statistics www.bls.gov

- Average workers 55 to 64 have tenure of 9.3 years. 25–34 have an average tenure of 2.9 years.[51]

- Perhaps the most daunting of these factors is the shrinking pool of potential management workers. The population of workers 30–44 is in decline, the generation of workers usually promoted into mid-management roles.

- Escalating health care costs are unsustainable. It will be years before the true cost savings of health care reforms are realized, and businesses and their employees will continue to absorb the burden. According to Towers Perrin, health care costs grew over 500% over the last two decades. Costs have escalated to $14,064 per family for the employer and $3,276 for the employee. Since 1999, the average US wage has increased 37%, while health care costs have gone up 151%. Employer costs going up faster than profits are a zero sum game.

- The U shape employment curve presents employers with the prospect of a larger group of older workers having to coexist with a group of younger ones. For the first time, we will have four generations of workers in the work force, a factor that will be the driver of massive change in the way we work.

At the very least, our economy faces the prospect of a significant labor imbalance in the decade ahead.

Thus, using strategic thinking and a scenario mindset, the convergence of all of these factors leads us to a momentous conclusion. In the next decade, those companies who are best-in-class employers will have a competitive advantage over those who are not.

A recent McKinsey study including 77 companies and over 6,000 managers concluded, "The most important corporate resource over the next 20 years will be talent; smart, sophisticated business people who are technologically literate, globally astute, and operationally agile."[52]

In the '50s and '60s, it was the product innovators that built shareholder value. In the '70s and '80s, we moved to the service economy.

Moving forward, it will be organizations that are able to attract talent that will be in the driver's seat in the experience economy. The winners in the talent war will be the ones who will have the resources to execute customer centric strategies.

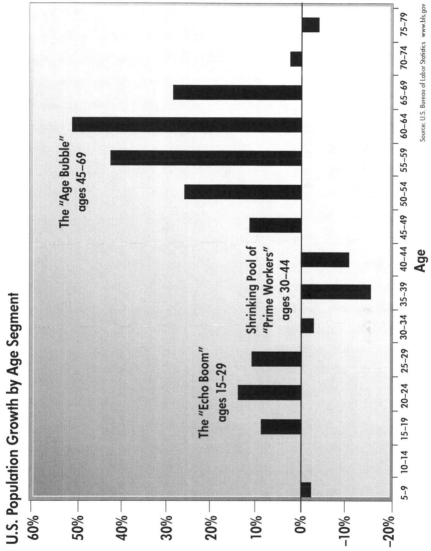

U.S. Population Growth by Age Segment

The "Age Bubble"
ages 45–69

Shrinking Pool of
"Prime Workers"
ages 30–44

The "Echo Boom"
ages 15–29

Age

Source: U.S. Bureau of Labor Statistics   www.bls.gov

Those organizations that create a superior level of engagement with employees are the most profitable. According to ISR Research, studies of "employee engagement" find that public companies who rate in the 75th percentile have 2.6 times the earnings per share growth rate of below average companies.[53]

The employment value proposition is changing, as employers must sweeten their offer if they want to retain the most talented employees. A paradigm shift is underway, where employers are recognizing that they must address employees' individual needs, much in the way marketers distinguish customer's individual needs. This presents a significant opportunity for dynamic employers, as employee satisfaction in the marketplace is so poor.

Every year the Gallup organization surveys over 100,000 US workers.[54] One of the questions asked of employees is if they are "engaged," meaning aligned with the mission and values of their respective organizations. On one recent survey 55% said no, 26% said yes, and 19% said that they were "actively disengaged," or working against their organizations (I refer to this as the Terrell Owens syndrome).

The hypercompetitive marketplace has created enormous price sensitivity and pressure on margins resulting in cost cutting, and the severing of millions of American jobs. The net result is a domino effect where there are less people doing more work (thus the higher output per US worker). These trends have put tremendous stress on the average worker.

The average US father spends only 4 minutes of meaningful interaction per day with his children. Sixty-five percent of workers are overweight and 69% have a sleep disorder.[55] Heart disease, hypertension and the degradation of our mental health are pervasive public health concerns. Work life balance has become a more prevalent issue, as workers seek a higher quality of life.

As the talent race evolves, employers are now creating "Employer Brands" and actively marketing themselves as employers of choice. Competitions such as Fortune magazine's 100 Best Companies to Work For and regional contests are sprouting up around the country as employers try to create a unique value proposition for employment.

Such employers are a magnet for talent; potential applicants gravitate toward them organically.

So how will employers provide employees a more meaningful work environment, and more time with their families while promoting more rigorous performance standards? The 4,000+ employees at Best Buy's corporate headquarters in Minneapolis, Minnesota were asked to take part in the company's "Results Oriented Work Environment" program. They were given complete latitude to design their work schedule. There were no meetings. Staff members could work any number of hours, as long as they met their performance objectives. The experiment has yielded extraordinary results including reduced turnover, higher job satisfaction and a 41% increase in productivity. Results Oriented Work Environments (ROWE) is not a feel-good management experiment, but an indication of a trend toward greater worker accountability.

The primary challenge for companies employing alternative work environments is not the productivity of workers but finding ways to keep off-site workers engaged. At Best Buy, employees participating in ROWE are required to come into the office once a week to reconnect with others and fortify their relationships.

> *The trend toward alternative work environments is both a cultural phenomenon and a management trend. Work is not a destination (a place you go to) but an activity (something you do).*

Traditional job roles have given way to flextime, telecommunicating, job sharing, consulting and outsourcing.

> *Managers are conditioned to observe activity, which explains our fascination with "work ethic," determined by how many hours an employee works or how many sales calls a salesperson makes.*

Often, executives are uncomfortable with alternative work arrangements. Managers accustomed to this approach are petrified that if they cannot see the employee, they will not be able to see productivity, or that the other employees may view the arrangement as favoritism.

People working from home are intuitively aware of this phenomenon. I would suggest that they overcompensate for it. One study revealed that the average virtual worker works 48 hours per week, compared to the average office employee who works 44, in part because they are not wasting time commuting to work. Generally, virtual workers are more productive, spend more time with their families, enjoy a better quality of life, and are less motivated to separate from their companies.

The search for balance, combined with new financial realities, shows a record number of women are re-entering the workforce after raising their kids. The most infamous of the "on-rampers" was Brenda Barns, former CEO of PepsiCo's North American operations. After a 6-year hiatus she returned as CEO of Sara Lee. Like senior workers, and Gen X's/Y's, stay-at-home moms and those re-entering the work force will seek flextime, telecommuting, compressed work weeks and part time work.[56]

> *Having to serve the varying needs of workers five decades apart in age will require that employers provide more options to employees in terms of benefits and working environment. One could easily challenge the logic of providing the same medical plan to a 22-year-old single male, and a 45-year-old female with a couple of kids at home (people in their 20s rarely go to the doctor at all).*

Cafeteria-style benefits have emerged, allowing employees to choose the benefits most relevant to them (equal to or below a maximum dollar amount). As the employment offer shifts, employers will design entire work environments (as in the case with Best Buy) that meet the dual objectives of serving customers and optimizing the employee experience.

Given the triple digit gain in health care inflation, employers are taking ownership of their employees' health (which was taboo just 10 years ago). With the advent of nursing lines, nutritional programs, flu vaccinations, elder care and health scans, employers are proactively investing in lowering their employees' health care risk.

Companies are retooling their benefits to create a differentiated offer. Consider some of the creative benefits offered by some predominant US employers:

- Onsite day care
  Compuware, Novant Health, Quad/Graphics
- Onsite pets
  Autodesk
- Onsite gourmet meals
  Analytic Graphics, SAS
- Onsite fitness center
  Northwestern Mutual Life, Progressive Insurance, Yankee Candle
- Subsidized vacations for all employees
  Homestead Technologies, S.C. Johnson & Son
- Incentives for buying a hybrid car
  Hyperion, Integrated Archive Systems, Timberland, Topics Entertainment
- Tuition reimbursement
  American Specialty Health, J. M. Smucker, Wegman's Food Markets
- Concierge service to run errands
  Chicago Children's Memorial Hospital, Norton Healthcare
- Sleep breaks at work
  Kaye/Bassman, Le Gourmet Gift Basket
- Internal Facebook connecting all employees
  Google
- Take home meals
  Fox Entertainment

❖   ❖   ❖

In my discussions with hundreds of CEOs about issues such as the multigenerational workforce, it is clear there is a perception that younger workers do not share the work ethic of their older counterparts. Yet given the employment U curve, employers will not only be forced to recruit young workers, they will have to integrate them with older ones as well. Younger workers have a different way of thinking about work and life, and employers will have to embrace a new ethos if they wish to engage them.

> *To understand the variant needs of these workers, it is important to understand their belief system, much of which was shaped in their youth.*

Baby Boomers, generally born before 1960, were connected to another time, experiencing the Great Depression and World War II through the stories of their parents and grandparents. They were accepting of institutions such as family, church and government. Their title at work was an important part of who they were.

The GenXers, those born in the '60s and '70s, grew up with different childhood memories, including Vietnam, the drug culture, the murders of JFK and MLK, and the suicides of idols like Janis Joplin and Jimi Hendrix. Their distrust of government reached a low during the Nixon years.

Gen Y, born in the period from roughly 1985–2000 lived through the Challenger accident, 9/11, scandals in the Catholic Church and Bill Clinton's presidency. They experienced a complete breakdown of American institutions and values. Thus, many do not share Baby Boomer patriotism or loyalty to their employers. They also grew up in the age of personal computing.

Where an older worker may be more apt to throw people at a problem, a Millennial (Y) will attempt to automate or leverage technology. While the old school manager wants to have a conversation, the Y will prefer a text or some other form of electronic communication (anyone with a teenager at home inherently understands this).

The disillusionment on the part of the Millennials has led to the need for independence combined with a thirst for being connected to something bigger than they are. This combination has been the inspiration for social networking sites and other emerging technologies. The most dynamic employers will use social networks to provide these workers a sense of community.

Younger workers, fueled by the expectations of their youth, show up to work with specific goals and expectations. They are accustomed to working in teams where diversity is celebrated.[57]

They multitask well and can manage multiple projects concurrently. They will prefer physical and/or electronic environments that enable collaboration. They will not understand the natural pecking order of the corporation.

Younger workers seek work experiences that lead to lateral career options, where exposure to various roles rounds out their resumes. These generational workers have different criteria for evaluating employers. Approximately 40% of Millennials will research a potential employer's commitment to environmental issues (green) on the employer's Web site. As many of the top business schools now utilize online and collaborative resources in their coursework, these workers are more adaptive to online resources.

In order to succeed in a workplace where the Xs and Ys are pushing the envelope, Baby Boomers will have to adapt to and embrace new technologies and workplace methods. Online training tools such as learning management systems will become more prevalent.[58]

❖   ❖   ❖

One can witness alignment on display as a passenger on Southwest Airlines. Founder Herb Kelleher said "Leadership is getting people to want to do what you want them to do because they share your purpose, vision and values. The people at Southwest Airlines work in relationships in which the role of the leader and collaborator are interchangeable. Our culture is our most valuable competitive market asset."

Southwest's culture was chronicled in the book *Nuts*:

Internal Spirit of Service

↓

Employee Satisfaction

↓

Retain Great People

↓

Employee Commitment Productivity

↓

Customer Satisfaction

↓

Customer Retention

↓

Value and Profit

SOUTHWEST'S VALUE DRIVERS
Source: *Nuts* by Jackie Freiberg

By creating an "Internal Spirit of Service," Southwest's management believes they will satisfy more customers, which will be the driver to "Value and Profit."

Southwest's operating results are beyond description. Their strategy is not complex: be the low-cost leader, fly only 737s, fly to offbeat underutilized airports. By turning the planes around quicker, Southwest is able to maintain higher asset utilization and lower cost per passenger mile over the life of each airplane. They have simply out executed the competition, in part because of superior employee engagement. I was once on a Southwest flight when the flight attendant came on the P.A. and said, "Ladies and gentleman, we are celebrating a birthday today. This gentleman is turning 100 years old today! Our pilot…"

On Southwest flights, it appears that the flight attendants and pilots are having fun. The contrast to employees of other carriers is striking. Some of the unionized flight attendants on other carriers look like they need an enema and openly criticize their employer in front of passengers.

> In Southwest's case, people are not just the ones that implement the strategy; they are the strategy.

Younger and older workers alike want to have fun and fun in the workplace is cheap. To regularly celebrate company accomplishments (such as having mariachi bands or pizza parties) requires much less investment than raising medical benefits by 1% and fun yields a higher return.

As the young guns in Silicon Valley have taught us, value today is measured in different terms and often the less rigid work environments yield a higher business valuation. Yet to have a Results Oriented Work Environment, you have to have … results.

In the case of small and medium sized organizations, the traditional corporate hierarchy may not promote positioning the senior HR executive in a strategic role. Often, the HR Director is an admin, promoted into a role where they had no formal training. Often, they report to the CFO, whose role it is to minimize costs and not to appreciate employees as human capital.

There is a strong correlation between the most profitable companies, and their human resources methodologies. The authors of *The HR Scorecard* conducted a study of more than 2,800 companies, and compared the HR best practices of the top 10% in terms of financial performance with the bottom 10%. The following table represents a comparison of various employment activities within these two groups:

	Bottom 10%	Top 10%
Sales per employee	**$ 158,101**	**$ 617,576**
Market value to book	3.6	11.1
% merit increase or incentives tied to performance	2%	87%
# of hours training — new employees	35	117
# of hours training — experienced employees	13	72
% of employees — regular performance appraisal	4%	95%

Source: *The HR Scorecard* by Becker, Huselid and Ulrich

The data makes a compelling case that the most profitable companies provide significantly more support in terms of on-boarding, training and performance management than poorly run organizations. Of the top performers, 95% provide a "regular performance review," compared to 4% for the poorer performers; a clear correlation. The top performing companies embrace performance cultures and hold people responsible to specific performance outcomes.

Throughout my career, I have observed a distinct difference in the way that companies manage performance. Performance reviews are a rare opportunity to create a dialog of complete candor, forcing people to be introspective and to create alignment with the values of the organization.

The ability to be completely candid goes against human nature. We are often overly polite and safe in our communication. Leaders want to be liked so they don't always address performance problems with the people who work for them. In such instances, silence is validation for sub-optimal behavior and performance. Conversely, highly effective leaders fight through these tendencies and put all of their cards on the table. Best-in-class companies have a methodical approach to performance management with the goal of managing succession in an intentional manner.

> *Great managers set very clear expectations for people. It is more intentional to tell people exactly what you expect of them than to discipline them for doing what you don't want.*

Senior managers are often confounded that employees do not understand what is expected of them. Even when a company's mission, values and strategies are clearly articulated, employees don't always understand why they are performing certain activities.

The objective of every performance review should be to discuss the specific performance of people against pre-determined goals. A great majority of those goals can be directly linked to strategic priorities. Goals should always meet the SMART criteria (specific, measurable, attainable, realistic and timely).

In 2003, Toyota set a stretch goal of 15% global market share by 2010.[59] As explained by Toyota President Fujo Cho, the goal was not meant to be a quantifiable budgetary goal, but a way to inspire employees. Such thinking is representative of a performance culture that has led Toyota to market leadership.

There is also a clear correlation between employee satisfaction and client satisfaction. Many of the companies who are on top of J.D. Power's Customer Satisfaction Index are also on the Fortune Magazine 100 Best Companies To Work For list.[60]

According to the American Society of Quality, the number one reason that customers change suppliers is "attitude of indifference on the part of the service provider" (68%), compared to dissatisfaction with product (14%) and lured away by competitor (9%).

Employers should offer an environment — including training, performance management and office design — that will support the business discipline and value proposition they wish to promote.

Finding people with the specific skill sets that employers desire will result in retention becoming a success factor. Turnover which averages about 17% nationally is a costly exercise.

Consider the cost of turnover among membership big box retailers (pre-recession). Walmart's Sam's Club warehouse stores are number two in market share, just trailing number one Costco. Costco pays an average wage of $17 per hour, while Sam's Club employees earn an average of $9.86 per hour (up to $11 in some markets).[61]

Less than half of Sam's Club employees are covered by health insurance, and on average, pay 33% of the premium, compared to the 82% of Costco workers, who on average pay 8%.

Want to guess who has higher turnover? Costco's turnover is estimated at 17% compared with Sam's Club at 44%. The hard cost of Sam's Club turnover is projected to be double that of Costco, more than offsetting any gains in cheaper wages.

> *Yet, the downside of turnover cannot be measured in tangible costs. The greater cost of severed employee relationships is the cost on alignment; losing the hearts and minds of those that are left behind.*

For a company of Costco's size, they have a unique corporate culture driven by their CEO Jim Sinegal. Sinegal visits up to a dozen stores per day, shaking hands with employees proudly wearing his Costco nametag which just reads "Jim." Jim also answers his own phone, and fields customer complaints personally. Instead of taking a multimillion-dollar salary, Sinegal pays himself $350,000 per year, allowing Costco to pay its employees more.

Sinegal's humble leadership approach and service orientation personifies the company. Costco is more like a family than a company, literally. Vice President of Bakery Susan MaConnaha is not shy about the organization. "My whole family works for Costco; my husband does, my daughter does, my new son-in-law does," she said.

Walmart has had to use bully tactics to avoid unionization. While Costco has the attention of the unions, it appears that their employees feel that they are getting a better offer.

Union membership in the US had been declining for 50 years from its peak of 28% of all employed in 1954 to less than 15% today, even though the average unionized worker makes 28% more for comparable work.[62] The Obama administration is clearly moving toward regulations that will make it easier for unions to infiltrate new businesses. Companies are clearly incented to improve working conditions to satisfy workers.

Chapter 13 Review

- There will be a massive global labor in-balance in the next 10 years.

- Companies who are best-in-class employers will have a competitive advantage over those who are not.

- Leading organizations recognize employee's individual needs and create a custom offer for compensation, benefits, etc.

- Best-in-class companies are a magnet, attracting the best talent.

- High profit companies provide more training and feedback to employees than lower performing companies.

Chapter

14

The Missing Piece:
Performance Management and
Pay for Performance

"High expectations are the key to everything."

— SAM WALTON

I am often amused by how much I learn raising my two beautiful daughters. Their rooms are full of trophies from childhood competitions in basketball, soccer and gymnastics. They worked hard for those trophies, but like all the other kids, the hardware was handed to them like candy on Halloween. In a world where they are coddled and driven to every practice, kids today are inbred with a sense of entitlement. We live in a world where every kid gets a trophy.

This behavior has crossed over into the workplace, where an epidemic of complacency and a lack of accountability are pervasive in our economy.

We work in an environment where managers and their employees expect a raise and a bonus on their anniversary date, regardless of their actual performance or results. Much of this behavior starts at the top.

Following the US government seizure of Fannie Mae and Freddie Mac in 2008, it took an act of Congress to protect the shareholders from paying outrageous salaries to executives who managed their businesses so poorly that they were driven into a takeover by the Federal government. And then there was the news of Merrill Lynch CEO John Thain spending millions of dollars redecorating his office, while the company was spinning out of control. The public has expressed its clear frustration with large payouts based on poor results.

There was a similar lack of responsibility at the C-Level of US automakers, whose arrogance was well published through their feeble attempt to access US subsidies while flying to Washington on three separate corporate jets. Executives making exorbitant salaries for performing well is one thing; being paid millions for losing money is another.

Conversely, Boeing CEO Jim McNerney is one of the country's most coveted executives. McNerney learned his craft under fire at GE, where he was a finalist for the CEO job that went to Jeff Immelt.

One of McNerney's strategies is to improve each employee's productivity by 15% each year.[63] Part of the performance culture at GE was created through vigilant individual measurement, a competency McNerney has brought to Boeing. The importance of productivity gains cannot be understated, as according to Peter Drucker and others, such increases have been the primary catalyst to the US economy and our extraordinary quality of life.

> *Thus, the science of hiring, retaining, and motivating is not a feel good exercise, but a material contributor to profitability.*

For companies like Boeing to increase productivity by 10–15%, organizations need to be able to measure the productivity of each employee in each and every year. Gaining engagement and holding people responsible is a required skill for the C-Level executive in the hypercompetitive marketplace.

As we have documented, best-in-class organizations are highly intentional in the practices around managing individual performance. Performance reviews should not be thought of as a meeting with a beginning and an end. They are an opportunity for setting forth a course for performance excellence. In lieu of measuring people based on the type of subjective measures in the typical performance review, best-in-class companies maintain very specific objectives with employees which are set in advance and reviewed regularly.

Often, goals are set top to bottom by management. Say your sales manager (let's call him John) hires a salesman for your company (Gary).

Given Gary's inexperience, John comes up with a sales budget for Gary. Using the sales of the prior sales rep in that territory as a baseline, they arrive at a sales forecast of 8% growth over the prior year.

Gary may not have felt that the goal was reasonable, but given his unfamiliarity with John, he accepted it anyway. Say that Gary achieved 4% growth in his territory, in his mind a positive result. He may be inclined to ask for a raise or bonus.

John tells Gary that he will not receive the bonus because Gary had not reached his sales budget. Gary tells John that given the environment, 8% was unreasonable. Manager's who fail to set clear expectations with people are often disappointed in the outcomes.

A poorly designed or executed performance management system can yield unintended consequences. Following is an example of a productive performance management cycle:

Having scorecards in place builds trust as employees feel more connected and informed about the corporate strategy. Individual goals should be a derivative of corporate objectives.

As illustrated in the *HR Scorecard* statistics, the more often communication occurs with an employee, the better he or she will perform. Say that you were traveling on business and were told of a path where you could go for a jog. A quarter mile into your run you sense you are lost and are redirected. You would get on track much faster than if you were corrected a mile later.

We advocate that one-to-ones occur between each manager and direct report at least one time per month. Often senior executives tell me that they utilize management by walking around. This is a good practice but people are not going to communicate with the same level of candor and specificity on the shop floor as they would in a thoughtfully orchestrated one-to-one session, where work goals are clearly identified, tracked and adjusted (when necessary).

> *To achieve peak performance, workers need to be provided candid feedback on their strengths and weaknesses and how they can improve their performance.*

Another best practice that enables communication is the use of self assessments. If the employee has a more elevated view of themselves than the employer, the gap must be closed or they will become dissatisfied with the lack of praise they receive.

> *The goal of any performance review should be gap closure; making sure that the employer and employee have the same view of the employee's performance.*

They will eventually become disenchanted and quit, or become disruptive (another illustration of the Terrell Owens syndrome).

Only through having the employee complete a self assessment, can you know if such a disconnect exists. When using a self assessment, the manager can consider the employee's opinions in writing the review, but ultimately the managers ratings are the ones that would be used for documentation and compensation purposes.

In BusinessWeek's 2009 Top 50 Best Performers Edition, the magazine found, "A common trait among companies on the list is that they pay for performance. Salaries may be stingy, but incentives are generous."

> *Every year, Bain and Company conducts a survey of CEO's to gauge ROI on management initiatives (such as activity based costing, Six Sigma and customer satisfaction surveys). Consistently, pay for performance yields the greatest impact on profitability.*

Incentives got a bad rap during the AIG debacle, but it was not incentives that were put on trial. It was bad incentives, paid out when companies were unprofitable, that were so controversial. In an age where accountability and transparency are more important than they have ever been, a company's incentive plan must be in alignment with the strategy and the behaviors the company is trying to reinforce.

Central to the design of a pay for performance is fairness. Consider some of the approaches used when incentives are not paid based on performance standards:

a) A company exceeds their profit targets, and pays a bonus to all employees, even those who have not pulled their weight or met performance targets.

b) A company does not meet its profit targets, but has exceptional performers who don't receive any bonuses or incentives.

c) A company meets its performance targets, but pays everyone the same incentives, regardless of their performance.

Pay for performance has been the source of debate in HR circles as companies grapple with the tension between treating everyone the same and rewarding those who have achieved the most. Paying bonuses to people who have not earned them is unfair to the employer and to the high achievers whose bonus opportunities are reduced (through opportunity cost).

In public companies, incentives are often tied to stock price, which is a slippery slope. If incentives are based on stock price alone, executives may make decisions based on short-term gains instead of long-term shareholder value. It is difficult for employees to directly control stock price. They have more tangible influence on variables such as margins, quality or client satisfaction. In order to mitigate these potential problems, we advocate a blended pay for performance model:

- Each employee receives an annual performance review and a score based on their ratings (which tend to be highly subjective). Based on their performance against the assessment criteria, the employee receives a cost of living adjustment and perhaps a raise based on their completion of tasks and projects that were pre-determined at the beginning of the year.

- At the end of the fiscal year, the employee is paid a bonus based on several buckets (usually 2–3, depending on how the plan is structured):

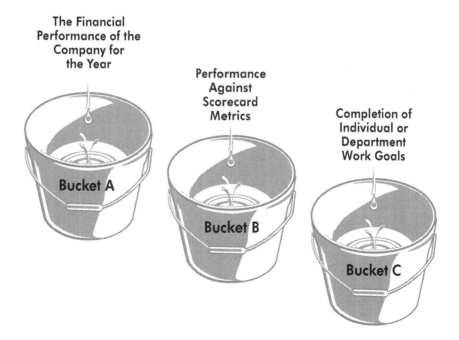

The Financial Performance of the Company for the Year — Bucket A

Performance Against Scorecard Metrics — Bucket B

Completion of Individual or Department Work Goals — Bucket C

Each bucket is weighted so that each section is relevant to the employee's position and ability to contribute to profitability. In some instances, minimum and maximum limits are set on the allowable bonus amount. There are relevant measurements for every employee including the receptionist and janitor.

The three buckets could be illustrated as follows:

Beginning:	04/01/2006
Ending:	03/31/2007
Base Salary:	$100,000
Allowable Bonus %:	10%

Weighting of Bonus Potential

Financial Indicators	:	50%
Scorecard Indicators	:	25%
Job Performance Indicators	:	25%

A simplified version of pay for performance would be to:

- Establish three or four objective measures for each employee that are pre-determinate before their performance cycle begins.
- Weight each measure.
- Review the goals with the employee in advance.
- Determine a bonus pool based on profitability.
- Allocate the pool, paying a percentage to each employee, factoring in their performance against the goals.

Financial Indicators (Actual Bonus Calculation)
Weight of this Section : 50%   Bonus Potential : $5,000
Must Equal .75 – 1.25

	Weight	Goal	Actual	Min	% Realized	Bonus Achieved
EBITDA % Increase	100%	10%	6%	8%	0%	$ 0 –
Bonus Achieved Financial						**$ 0**

Scorecard Indicators (Actual Bonus Calculation)
Weight of this Section : 25%   Bonus Potential : $2,500
Must Equal .75 – 1.33

	Weight	Goal	Actual	Min	% Realized	Bonus Achieved
Customer Service up sell percent	50%	50%	53%	53%	100%	$1,250
New Customers Acquired	50%	3,600	3,844	98%	100%	$1,250
Bonus Achieved Scoreboard						**$2,500**

Job Performance Indicators (Actual Bonus Calculation)
Weight of this Section : 25%   Bonus Potential : $2,500
Must Equal .75 – 1.25

	Weight	Goal	Actual	Min	% Realized	Bonus Achieved
Integrate with cost system by 06/01/08	50%	Y/N	Yes		100%	$1,250
Hire 5 qualified CS reps and train by 12/01/08	50%	Y/N	No		0%	$ –
Bonus Achieved Job Performance						**$1,250**

Total Bonus Achieved	**$3,750**

And now, an explanation on why I am fascinated with Terrell. Of all the athletes in modern day sports, Terrell Owens is among the most controversial. There is a media storm wherever he goes, covering whatever he does. Owens is a tremendous physical specimen; a raw combination of power, explosiveness and speed.

In 2004, Owens wore out his welcome in San Francisco, where his on-field and off-field antics led to a trade by the 49ers to the Baltimore Ravens for whom he refused to play. His rights were then traded again to the Philadelphia Eagles. During the ensuing season, T.O. (as he refers to himself in the third person) was the leading receiver on a team that went to the Super Bowl.

During the season, T.O. had several confrontations with his quarterback Donovan McNabb and his coach Andy Reid. Owens then suffered a serious injury, and was expected to miss the playoffs. T.O., utilizing his own medical staff and an oxygen chamber designed to rehabilitate his ailing leg, came back in miraculous fashion to play in Super Bowl XXXIX against the New England Patriots. The Eagles lost, a defeat T.O. blamed on his quarterback.

During the following season, the war of words continued in the press. With T.O. becoming a constant distraction, the team released him in mid-season.

The following year, T.O. was signed by the Dallas Cowboys. The team turned into a circus. T.O. missed most of training camp with a hamstring injury, opting to use his own trainers instead of the team's specialists. Knowing that every television network was covering his exploits on a daily basis, he smiled for the cameras riding a stationary bike. One day, he wore a Discovery Team bicycle jersey and helmet, as if to mock the entire process, and provide a disgusting comparison to Lance Armstrong.

He spent the next few weeks complaining about his role in the offense before an incident where paramedics were summoned to his home when he apparently suffered a reaction to supplements he was taking. Rumors (never proven to be true) that he attempted suicide completely consumed the Cowboys and talk radio. T.O. was a distraction again.

In the two seasons to follow, the Dallas Cowboys, considered by many as the most talented team in the National Football League, underperformed. Every time T.O. was admonished by the press, the team's owner Jerry Jones came to his defense. Finally, the Cowboys released him in 2009.

Terrell Owens is a remarkably talented man, who has no concept of teamwork or the greater good. He is like a cancer on every team he plays for. Most work environments have a T.O. They are the ones who are "needed" because of a particular competency, relationship with customers or other value their employer holds dear. As one NFL general manager put it, "When you bring in drama queens, you get drama."

Unfortunately, cancers tend to spread. The longer the cancer has to spread, the harder it is to control and the longer it takes to cure. The costs are enormous, both in terms of hard costs and loss of morale and engagement.

In some cases, employers are hesitant to terminate employees because they fear litigation. Some employees take advantage of liberally written labor laws and manipulate the system. These employees are like terrorists in the drive for alignment, using unconventional and desperate measures to sabotage the efforts of their employers. The only thing worse than an employee who quits and leaves, is an employee who quits and stays.

I once did some pro bono work for a non-profit client. Management was struggling with what to do about a branch manager who had clearly become disruptive. He had caused massive turnover and had challenged the organization's values with his unethical behavior.

The managing director was concerned that a termination would almost certainly bring about a nasty labor action, given comments made by this individual in the past. I suggested that the organization consult with their labor attorney, gather all the necessary documentation (to ensure a legal separation) and quantify the risk of any legal liability and legal fees. When I pressed the client on what a lawsuit might cost them, their estimate was $30,000. I asked, "What would it cost you to keep him?" The client concluded that keeping the cancer would cost much more than $30,000.

There is a fine line between being a conscientious manager who cares about people deeply, and a soft one that accepts mediocrity or poor performance. The number one thing that organizations must do to optimize performance and ensure the execution of strategy is to eliminate poor performers.

Chapter 14 Review

- Pay for performance is proven to provide a high return on investment.

- Incentives should be tied to strategic priorities through scorecards or other measurement systems.

- Blend metrics that reward both company profitability and individual contributions.

Chapter

15

The End Game

It's far better to buy a wonderful company at a fair price than a fair company at a wonderful price.

— Warren Buffett

I am a hopeless entrepreneur; and will always want to be part of the chase. But most business owners visualize an exit or liquidity event as the end game. Often such transactions lead to extraordinary material wealth, and validate the entrepreneurs' years of sweat equity.

> *Business owners dream their entire careers of such an event, but few have a thorough understanding of the mechanics of a sale.*

This chapter serves as a guideline on how to convert your life's work into a liquidity transaction.

Given the lofty multiples (of EBITDA—Earnings Before Interest, Taxes, Depreciation and Amortization) paid in recent years, we have seen numerous clients see big paydays. Those who follow the formula laid out in the preceding pages have realized more business value than those who have run their businesses more haphazardly.

> *While such a transaction can be a defining event in one's life, the business owner must always question if the grass is really greener on the other side.*

A transaction may provide for a better lifestyle and less investment risk. But the entrepreneur must weigh the benefits against both the hard costs and opportunity costs. Earning a 10% or 20% return in a business is practically impossible to replicate in stocks, bonds or fixed securities.

Selling a growing business prematurely creates a double whammy; a lower profit number on which the multiple is based and lower investment income earned on the proceeds post transaction (after taxes). The following table illustrates the difference in the value of a business based on several scenarios:

Revenue	$30M	$35M	$35M	$40M	$40M
EBITDA	$3.00M	$3.50M	$5.25M	$6.00M	$6.00M
EBITDA %	10%	10%	15%	15%	15%
Multiple	5	5	6	6	7
Enterprise Value	$15.0M	$17.5M	$31.5M	$36.0M	$42.0M

Thus, growing a business from $30 million in sales to $40 million, while increasing EBITDA from 10% to 15% and achieving a 7x multiple (in lieu of a 5x multiple) results in a whopping 113% increase in value.

The shrewd seller works tirelessly to optimize the value of the business years before entering the fray of mergers and acquisitions (M&A). Many business decisions (such as, who to hire and which capital improvements to make) may be influenced by the affect on a sale in the years to come.

Once the decision to sell is made, the entrepreneur must brace for impact. The level of commitment required to divest a business is extraordinary. A CEO could spend 50% of his bandwidth for 6 months or more to affect a transaction. The burden on the CFO and his or her staff could be even more intrusive.

Any business owner wishing to enter into such a transaction must surround himself with a cadre of seasoned advisors. In a world full of sharks, those with the sharpest bite swim in the world of M&A, and failure to prepare for entrance into the tank can be costly.

Some larger companies have outside teams tasked with assisting internal transaction teams to prepare for a sale. To level the playing field, the business owner should have a Board of Directors or Board of Advisors to guide them during the process and assist in the selection of the transaction team including; an investment banker, CPA and legal counsel. A Board of Advisors or Board of Directors can act as a counter-balance to the weight of a professional private equity buyer and their transaction professionals.

Often attorneys and CPAs will represent to their clients that they can manage such transactions. Only service professionals who are M&A specialists should be considered for such roles. CPAs provide independent financial information in the form of review or audit (often three years of data). A good transactional attorney will draft various agreements and may provide other counsel such as regulatory advice to the transaction team.

It is critical that advisors have no conflicts of interests. In the case of a banker, routinely representing buyers within a particular market space is an inherent conflict because the banker may have relationships that influence their thinking or could cause them to guide assets toward investors who they hope to deal with in the future.

> *M&A advisors are very, very expensive, and the good ones are worth every dime. Like hiring senior level talent, the selection of advisors should be conducted with patience and precision.*

Perhaps the most important decision in a sale is selection of the right investment banker. As outlined previously an investment banker that secures a price premium could easily deliver millions of dollars in incremental value. Evaluating bankers is not the time to be impatient or cheap.

Investment bankers are a different breed, and they often come with varying perspectives on how to manage a deal. For example, some will cast a wide net and talk to hundreds of potential buyers and others will use a more intimate approach based on very specific targets. The selling process is highly dynamic and the entrepreneur must be constantly available during various phases of the transaction.

The banker's role is to facilitate the sales process to completion. Steps may include:

- Extensive due diligence on the market and company
- Providing a "fair value" opinion based on converging factors (non- binding)
- Developing a finance structure and providing access to debt financing (when appropriate)
- Preparation of teaser materials for distribution to a targeted list of buyers
- Collaboration with a transactional attorney to create non-disclosure agreement (NDA) and other relevant documents
- Creation of a password protected "data room" were potential buyers can access information
- Preparing executives for management presentations
- Preparation of a "pitch book"
- Reviewing "Indication of Interest" letters
- Preparation (with attorney) of purchase agreement
- Facilitating management visits with targeted buyers
- Reviewing formalized letters of intent
- Negotiating on behalf of the seller
- Closing the transaction

It is the banker's job to create competition through a tightly controlled process that moves the most aggressive buyers through the funnel. Aggressive buyers will try to preempt the others through "exclusive" offers. Accepting such terms dissuades other bidders from spiking the value of bids. Exclusives tend to dilute the selling price and should be avoided unless the seller's objective is a speedy close.

During the selling process, bankers weed out potential buyers (based on their ability and willingness to pay), through Indication of Interest (IOIs), management visits and final offers. Once the seller targets a buyer who has provided a satisfactory offer and is likely to close, the banker facilitates due diligence and final contract negotiations. Like an inspection on a realty transaction, the buyer may discover problems and leverage them to try to discount the clearing price.

To earn your business, Investment Bankers are accustomed to participating in "bake offs" where they make formal presentations to a Board or senior management team. Presentations focus on the operating environment, company's value and how to position within the market.

Fees paid in a transaction can be as high as 5% of the purchase price. To sell a small/mid-market company, it is not uncommon for the investment banker to earn a $1 million fee and for accounting and attorney's fees to be several hundreds of thousands of dollars. Fees are typically capped and include a "get out" clause if the transaction does not close (it is very common that businesses offered to the market never close).

> There are two types of buyers: strategic and financial. A strategic buyer may have an interest in acquiring an asset because they perceive it to be synergistic with other businesses they own. A financial buyer views the business as a stand-alone entity that will generate cash in the future.

There are many forms of transactions such as: leveraged buyouts (LBOs), reverse leveraged buyouts, and management buyouts (MBOs), but we won't study their technical mechanics here. If you are a small or mid-market business owner, what is important to know is that a deal may be completed with leverage (debt financing), cash or equity.

Marketing a business to strategic buyers and financial buyers requires a slightly different strategy, but the fundamental value drivers that increase a company's value are fundamentally the same. Investors such as private equity firms are typically interested in:

- **Growth Story** — How has the business grown, and how will it continue to grow in the future? Is the market growing and what about the market, external factors and business assumptions are likely to change? What is the likelihood that the company can grow its share and profitability?

- **Management Team** — How strong is the management team and how likely are the members of it likely to stay should a transaction close? The strength of the management team is generally less important in the case of a strategic transaction when the investor is likely to consolidate support functions such as accounting and marketing, and eliminate such positions.

- **Cash Flow** — The ability of a business to generate cash is the primary determinant of value. Buyers and investment banks study cash flow analysis with rigor and scrutiny.

- **Margins** — How realistic are future margins, and how sheltered are they to outside threats such as increases to raw materials prices?

- **Customer Concentration** — Buyers are particularly attentive to customer concentration and which customers could be a flight risk. As value is calculated based on future cash flow, it is assumed in most industries that future revenue will be generated by current customers. There is generally a tolerance of 30 to 40% of volume with any customer or tightly defined segment.

Market intelligence is just as critical for a seller as it is for the buyer. The seller must ask; who are the potential targets and what are their reasons for buying? These variables need to be understood in advance, and require painstaking dedication and research. While bankers will provide valuation ranges, the reality is that the market dictates the value of a business, and no one really knows what the market will bear.

The most accepted method for valuation is a combination of comparable market multiples and discounted cash flows. The value of a business is based on a multiple of what future cash the business will generate after the net present value of money and discounts for macro, industry or company specific risks are considered. The science of applying the multiple to past (and potentially future) cash flows is subject to some interpretation, and negotiation.

The value of a company is derived through a bizarre combination of the known and unknown, and positive and negative attributes. If a business is not well operated, its deficiencies may diminish value, or a buyer may believe that application of new processes, technologies, management or synergies with other businesses could improve cash flow and drive up future value.

Private equity firms have a reputation for being brutish and demanding in their treatment of the management of companies they acquire. They expect structure and precision in the portfolio businesses they operate and often appoint board members and senior executives to govern. But private equity principals bring more to the table than their cash, egos and eagerness for growth.

Like investment bankers, these shrewd investors offer peripheral vision on industries and markets, a wealth of management experience and remarkable access to resources.

During the recession that began in 2008, private equity sat on the sidelines, waiting for the storm to blow over. According to the *Pregin Report,* private equity firms held $1 Trillion in "dry powder" (uncommitted assets) as of August, 2009.

As private equity firm's primary revenue is generated by "management fees" charged to businesses they own, their capital must be deployed for them to earn a profit. Many Fortune 500 companies also waited out the downturn and are flush with cash, which is material to smaller companies because greater activity will drive up multiples for both public and private company transactions.

A new cycle of acquisitions is on the horizon.

Some business owners are skittish about including key employees in the preparatory stages of a transaction out of fear that they may flee. While the word getting out is a legitimate concern, it is nearly impossible to contain the activities of the transaction team. Investment Bankers and buyers need information on every facet of a business, and the financial due diligence can be extreme. The invasion of Investment Bankers and buyers is difficult to disguise for long.

Proactive business owners provide senior managers retention packages, which are incentives designed to retain key talent and vest should a transaction be executed.

Generally, retention packages have a clause that void the incentive if the employee reveals the nature of the provision or the intentions to sell. The employee is guaranteed to realize a substantial bonus (a year's salary or more) if a transaction of a certain value is completed. The provision can include partial payment by the selling entity and guarantees for employment with additional payment by the buying entity (thus defraying part of the cost to the buyer).

Another reason for including management early in the process is to motivate them for the management presentation phase, which is a critical determinant of value. Management presentations (to buyers) are long, arduous and exhausting and by having skin in the game, the team is incented to perform well.

The challenges of selling a business cannot be understated. It is like being in a sprint and a marathon simultaneously. The risk of an unsuccessful transaction is high. Damage to a reputation can be costly with customers, vendors and especially to employees.

The upside can also be the culmination of a lifetime of blood, sweat and tears and result in extraordinary wealth.

Chapter 15 Review

- While a liquidity event may be an entrepreneur's defining business moment, it can also be a letdown.

- In selling a business it is crucial that the entrepreneur seek out quality advice from boards, investment bankers, CPAs and attorneys. Seek out M&A experts.

- Buyers will consider a broad range of business risks and will meticulously dissect business operations and financials.

- A new wave of acquisitions is imminent.

- Use incentives to retain key talent.

Chapter

16

Conclusion: Be Intentional

*"It's what you learn after you
know it all that counts."*

— JOHN WOODEN

John Crowley was running out of time. He had two children who were stricken with Pompe disease, a degenerative and fatal genetic condition. Crowley, formally an executive with Bristol Myers Squibb, faced the reality that there was no cure, and it was unlikely that Megan and Patrick would make it to their sixth birthdays.[64]

During Crowley's research, he came across Novazyme Pharmaceuticals Inc., a start up developing treatments for rare diseases such as Pompe. Novazyme, the brainchild of scientist William Canfield, was having difficulty raising money. So Crowley, desperate to save his children, quit his high paying job to become CEO of Novazyme.

As told by Geeta Anand in her inspirational book titled *The Cure*, early attempts to raise venture capital were rebuffed by a pharmaceutical establishment that was not accepting of fast track, come-to-market strategies. Larger pharmaceutical companies did not want any part of Novazyme or experimental therapies that reached a small group of patients. Researchers questioned the organization's claims and dismissed its practices.

At one point, to make payroll, Crowley took a second mortgage on his house. Through private donations, the company mustered up $300,000, enough to employ a group of researchers and begin plans to launch clinical trials on the company's breakthrough cache of drugs.

In order to create ownership and a sense of urgency among Novazyme employees, Crowley held "lunch and learns" with patients stricken with the disease. Every employee from the chief researcher to the junior staff took part. The experience created clarity and determination in a group of people for whom failure was not an option.

Lindsey Easton had beaten the odds, surviving Pompe until the age of 12. She visited Novazyme employees regularly, sharing her pain and suffering. She became a barometer of the company's success, and all of the people who worked there knew that it was unlikely that she would have a "sweet 16" party or graduate from high school.

Crowley and the employees of Novazyme persevered. They worked long hours, and met the demands of the FDA and a highly fickle and bureaucratic medical community.

Crowley convinced Neose Technologies to invest in Novazyme, providing a $27 million cash infusion and seed money for another start up, Amicus Therapeutics, which has established new treatments to address similar conditions. Novazyme built a new production facility in Lindsey's honor. She graduated from high school: Valedictorian. Novazyme is now charging the hill trying to find the cure. Megan and Patrick are still alive as of this writing and were the inspiration to the movie "Extraordinary Measures."

People are capable of amazing things when they have clarity of purpose, when they are inspired and engaged, and when they have an emotional attachment to the outcome. The employees of Novazyme were highly intentional in everything they did.

❖   ❖   ❖

I was enthralled by a keynote given by Lance Armstrong at a conference several years ago. He told the story of his rise to prominence as the world's premier cyclist. Having had cancer spread throughout his body, he had brain surgery in an Indianapolis hospital.

The day after the surgery, he was visited by his agent, who is one of his closest friends. When the agent asked him how he was doing, Armstrong said he was incredible (I am paraphrasing). The agent, befuddled by his state of mind fired back, "Lance, you almost died, how can you be so positive?" "I am low as you can go. It can only get better from here. I am going to reinvent myself," said Armstrong.

And he did. He went to the only race team that would have him and rebuilt the organization including a new team, equipment, sponsors and training regimen from scratch.

The Tour de France (cycling 2,200 miles through the Alps) is among the world's most grueling sporting events. Armstrong's feat of winning seven Tour De France titles in a row may be the most incredible sports achievement of our lifetime.

Many of us have our own mountains to climb, but we don't have to wait until we hit rock bottom to do it. We should be reinventing ourselves and our companies every day. Our clients expect it. Global hyper-competition requires it. To re-imagine your business requires the discipline and focus of a world champion bike racer. What will you reinvent today?

I believe in a principle I refer to as the 5% Rule. The difference between success and failure is a thin line. In baseball, the .225 hitter lives in anonymity at the end of the bench. The .275 hitter starts, hits in the meat of the lineup and makes a lot of money. When reduced to the single variable of hitting, the difference in their performance is 5%.

But those who rise above and give 5% more seem to get a payoff. It seems that the people who are most intentional in their actions reap the rewards of a more fulfilling quality of life. We do what we have to do, so that we can do what we want to do.

Work ethic alone is not the ticket. I once worked with a very driven man (I will call him Gary). It seemed that Gary wanted to engage in a contest of who could be most committed, which in his mind meant coming in the most Saturdays and working the most hours. He ate badly, did not exercise and was constantly stressed. Worse than that, he created stress for the people around him, many of whom found him overly intense and overbearing (unintended consequences). The yield of all his activity was not everything it could have been. He didn't seem to have clarity of purpose and there were diminishing returns on the energy he expended.

Many people are searching for balance in their life but they don't know where to find it. I take pride in referring to myself as a recovering workaholic. I rarely work because I have to; I work because I feel inspired. Consulting does offer a unique lifestyle, but the idea which was formed earlier about providing more freedom in the workplace is a reflection of my own experience and the difference it has made to my productivity. I believe I am immensely productive because I work on my terms, and not within the confines of an arbitrary schedule or work environment.

Our paradigm about work and our production has to change. The digital revolution affords us new flexibility to work how we want, when we want. I am simply smarter at 7 a.m. than at 5 p.m. which is why I am in the office every morning by 7 a.m. Why would an employer want to take someone with my body chemistry and force me into an arbitrary schedule (9–5)?

It takes discipline to maintain this schedule, but being intentional about time management and purposeful about my family life is the choice I have made. Your schedule may look very different, but the point is that you have to have one that suits you.

> *When people are more balanced at home, they are more intentional at work.*

When you are getting enough sleep, exercise, nutrition, and yes love, you perform better in the office. Given the impending labor in-balance, we need to change our view of employment and be intentional about how we provide employees a quality of life.

I have offered some conclusions about what the future might look like and how our business world may change. Regardless of what the future may bring there are some simple principles that work in almost any business, in any industry regardless of the economy or other external factors.

People who have specific objectives in their lives have a clearer picture of what they wish to achieve and how they will achieve it:

- Set a target valuation for your business and have a clear exit strategy.
- Name a successor years in advance, teach them the business and put them in a position to succeed.
- Set up date nights monthly with your spouse.

- Pay yourself first; schedule the time to attend your children's practices and recitals.
- Have a bucket list.
- Have a Board of Advisors/Directors who will challenge your assumptions.
- Set clear goals for your company one, three and five years in advance.
- Complete a strategic plan annually. Analyzing two or three scenarios that could affect your business.
- Convert the strategy into a corporate scorecard.
- Articulate your strategies, goal and metrics to all employees.
- Require salespeople to save all sales information and business intelligence into a CRM system.
- Have a clear marketing plan and cohesive Internet strategy.
- Maintain price integrity, even when business is soft.
- Survey clients and measure loyalty on an ongoing basis.
- Have a robust performance management system and make sure that performance reviews are done on time.
- Make sure every employee has set goals and has a training plan for the upcoming year.
- Have written procedures so that you can cover any job (when people are on vacation, or separate).
- Tell people what you expect from them.

In our over caffeinated, frantic environment, those people who are intentional and have some sense of purpose are distinctive. Being intentional translates into higher fees for our firm. I manage my time carefully, because I place a value on it.

If you don't value your time, no one else will.

Have you ever noticed that the people who seem like they should have the least time, actually have the most? They are often the ones that invest more heavily in productive administrative assistants, who make it to meetings on time and return your phone calls.

I challenge you to challenge your own assumptions:

* Why do your customers value your product or service?
* What would happen if you raised your prices by 10% across the board? How many of them would leave?
* If your business was new, would you enter that market again? What could change?
* What new businesses could you be in?
* If there were a catastrophic event, could your business survive? Could it run without you?
* Why do your employees work for you?
* Is your work schedule consistent with having a balanced life? How should it change? What are you going to do about it?

Now is the time to ask such questions of yourself and of your team. Now is the time to reinvent your business. Now is the time to gain alignment among your employees, and share in the fruits of your success.

The best-in-class companies we have referenced such as GE, Walmart and Southwest continuously improve. They are not satisfied with the status quo, and neither should you be. To stand still is to fall behind.

It is difficult to challenge your underlying assumptions, formed in your youth and reinforced over a lifetime of experiences. I am a member of Vistage (formally TEC), well known as the world's largest CEO membership organization. Being in a peer group is extraordinarily useful. It is a venue for like-minded professional people to serve as an advisory board to one another. The diversity of thought that occurs among people of different backgrounds, cultures and industries is rich and robust. For professionals interested in continuous improvement for themselves and their companies, such organizations are extraordinarily beneficial.

I am often amused when a new member joins our group because the concept of the unbridled truth, shared in a safe haven with complete trust and confidentiality, is in sharp contrast to the way that people typically interact. Peer groups are not for everyone, but meaningful relationships with advisors should be.

The most successful entrepreneurs are often the same ones who are open to counsel from outsiders. They embrace diversity of thought as fuel for their businesses, and leverage the energy of outside influences to shape their thinking. To accept advice from other people requires the admission that you don't have all the answers yourself. None of us do, and the faster we come to that realization, the more successful we will be. Given the rate of change and hyper-competitive marketplace, every business owner needs a Board of Directors, or less formal Board of Advisors.

It is a choice to be purposeful in our life. We must all wrestle with the challenge of what legacy we wish to leave.

> *It is one thing to build an enterprise that provides us wealth and prosperity, and another to make a lasting impression on the world through the people we inspire, the employees we develop, the products we produce, and the community we serve.*

We all have different priorities in life, but those who seem happiest are answering to a higher calling, whether it be time with their loved ones, a lifestyle they enjoy, or satisfying their religious convictions. Running a purposeful business is an enabler to these pursuits.

Alignment and accountability within an organization result from the sense of purpose orchestrated by its leaders. If you are intentional about your work, so will your employees. Organizations take on the personality traits of the people who lead them.

We have all seen people who seem to have it all; success, happiness, health and beautiful families who love them. They seem to be the same people with a plan. They are the ones who know exactly what they want and how to get it. Captain Sully Sullenberger would tell you that to live a purpose-driven life requires commitment and focus; and that it is worth it.

In your business and in your life, people will pay attention to how you show up. If you are confident and optimistic about creating the future you want, you will bring a lot of people along for the ride; those who seek intended consequences.

Chapter 16 Review

* Be intentional

ABOUT THE AUTHOR

Marc Emmer is President of Optimize Inc., a Valencia, California based management consulting firm. Marc is sought after by CEOs as a trusted advisor and expert in strategy, performance management and client satisfaction. Marc's specialty is strategic planning and implementing scorecarding methodologies in small and medium sized companies.

Marc has been active on the US speaking circuit with organizations such as Vistage, Renaissance Forums, The Association for Corporate Growth, and PIHRA and serves on four Boards of Directors.

Marc can be reached at *marc@optimizeinc.net*
For bookings contact *info@optimizeinc.net*

Large quantities of this book can be purchased at *www.optimizeinc.net/ic*

Single copies are available at *www.amazon.com* and at *www.createspace.com/10000251217*

www.optimizeinc.net

❖   ❖   ❖

Special Thanks

The publication of this work could not have been possible without the council and advice of Henry DeVries of The New Client Marketing Institute.

Henry can be reached at *henry@newclientmarketing.com*

Index

References

1   Yahoo Finance
2   "The Decent of Finance" by Niall Ferguson — *Harvard Business Review,* July 2009
3   "The Institutional Yes Interview" with Jeff Bezos — *Harvard Business Review,* October 2007
4   ibid.
5   "The Black Swan" by Nassim Nicholas Taleb — *Random House,* 2007
6   ibid.
7   *The Washington Post* — "Side Effect" by Margaret Webb Pressler, April 10, 2005
8   *The Ascent of Money* by Niall Ferguson — Penguin Press 2008
9   "The Netbook Effect" by Clive Thomson — *Wired* March 2009
10 *The Fourth Turning* by William Strauss and Neil Howe — Broadway Books, 1999
11 *Animal Spirits* by George Akerlof and Robert Shiller — Princeton University Press, 2009
12 "What DuPont Did Right," Ram Charan, book excerpt from *Leadership in the Era of Economic Uncertainty,* 2009
13 20 Forecasts for the Next 25 Years — World Future Society
14 "Solar Goes Supernova" by Chris Turner — Fast Company, November 2008
15 "Integrated Business Planning" — River Logic Planning Series, 2008
16 "How can Tibal Fisher Stores improve its Customer Research Process" — *Harvard Business Review,* August 2008

17 "A Designer Takes on His Biggest Challenge Ever" by Linda Tischler — Fast Company, February 2009

18 *Get There Early* by Bob Johansen Berrett — Loehler Publishers, 2007

19 *Profit or Growth* by Bala Chakavarthy and Peter Lorange — Wharton School Publishing, 2007

20 "Strategy Maps" by Robert Kaplan and David Norton — Harvard Business Press, 2004

21 The Next Global Stage by Kenichi Ohmae — Wharton School Publishing, 2005

22 "Outsmart" by Jim Champy — FT Press, 2008

23 Quick MBA at www.quickmba.com

24 "Firms More Prone to Go Vertical" — WSJ 11/30/09 — Bloomberg News

25 *Making Strategy Work* by Lawrence Hrebiniak — Wharton School Publishing, 2005

26 *The Growth Gamble* by Andrew Campbell and Robert Park — Nicholas Brealey Publishing, 2005

27 *The Walmart Effect* by Charles Fishman — Penguin Books, 2006

28 ibid.

29 US Department of Transportation Air Travel Consumer Report, April 2009

30 "Thinking Outside the Big Box" by Jeff Chu and Kate Rockwood — Fast Company, November 2008

31 *The Power of Personal Branding* by Tim O'Brien — Mendham Publishing, 2007

32 *Extreme Toyota* by Emi Osono, Norihiko Shimizu, and Hirotaka Takeuchi — John Wiley & Sons, 2008

33 "Retail Forward Shopper Scape" — *BusinessWeek,* June 15, 2009

34 "Strategies to Fight Low-cost Rivals" by Nirmalya Kumar — *Harvard Business Review,* December 2006

35 Yahoo Finance

36 "Strategies to Fight Low-cost Rivals" by Nirmalya Kumar — *Harvard Business Review,* December 2006

37 Adapted from *The Blue Ocean Strategy* by Chan Kim and Renee Mauorgne — Harvard Business School Press, 2005

38 Hanging Tough by Peter Mitchell SVP Wells Fargo

39 "Coach's New Bag" by Susan Berfield — *BusinessWeek,* June 29, 2009

40 "BCG Value Science Bloomberg Financial Markets, Boston Consulting Group, Compustat, Reuters," as printed in *BusinessWeek* Indata, September 22, 2008

41 Adapted from *The Experience Economy* by Joseph Pine and James Gilmore, 1999

42 Wikipedia Pepsi Challenge

43 Wikipedia at http://en.wikipedia.org/wiki/Strategy

44 "The Unique Advantage" by Alexander Kandybin & and Surbhee Grover — *Strategy & Business Autumn*, 2008

45 "To Get Value from a Merger Grow Sales" by Juergen Rothenuecher and Joerg Schrottke — *Harvard Business Review*, May 2008

46 "Seize Advantage in a Downturn" by David Rhodes and Daniel Stelter *Harvard Business Review*, February 2009

47 *Driving Change* by Mike Brewster and Fredrick Dalzell — Hyperian Publishing, 2007

48 "The Strategy-Focused Organization" by Robert Kaplan and David Norton — Harvard Business School Publishing, 2001

49 "Strategy Maps" by Robert Kaplan and David Norton — Harvard Business Press, 2004

50 "Turnover Difference" by Roland Beech, founder of TwoMinuteWarning.com

51 The US Bureau of Labor Statistics

52 "The War for Talent" by Charles Fishman *Fast Company*, December 2007

53 ISR Research

54 Gallup Poll

55 *The 500 Year* by Jim Taylor and Watts Wacker — HarperCollins, 1998

56 *Womenomics* by Claire Shipman and Katty Kay, HarperCollins, 2009

57 *Generations At Work* by Ron Zemke, Claire Raines, and Bob Filipczak — AMA Publications, 1999

58 Association For Training and Development Industry, November 2008

59 "Fortune Magazine's 100 Best Companies to Work For," 2009

60 ibid.

61 "The High Cost of Low Wages" by Wayne Cascio — *Harvard Business Review*, December 06

62 "What Role Will Unions Play in 2009" by Douglas Klein — *Talent Management Magazine*, April 2009

63 *You Can't Order Change* by Peter S. Cohan — The Penguin Group, 2008

64 Adapted from *The Cure* by Geeta Anand, 2006

NOTES

Made in the USA
Charleston, SC
20 July 2012